First World War
and Army of Occupation
War Diary
France, Belgium and Germany

60 DIVISION
179 Infantry Brigade
London Regiment
2/14 Battalion
1 January 1915 - 30 November 1916

WO95/3030/4

The Naval & Military Press Ltd
www.nmarchive.com
Published in association with The National Archives

Published by

The Naval & Military Press Ltd

Unit 10 Ridgewood Industrial Park,

Uckfield, East Sussex,

TN22 5QE England

Tel: +44 (0) 1825 749494

www.naval-military-press.com

www.nmarchive.com

This diary has been reprinted in facsimile from the original. Any imperfections are inevitably reproduced and the quality may fall short of modern type and cartographic standards.

© Crown Copyright
Images reproduced by permission of The National Archives, London, England, 2015.

Contents

Document type	Place/Title	Date From	Date To
Heading	WO95/3030/4		
Heading	60th Division 179th Infy Bde 2-14th Bn London Regt 1915 Jan-1916 Nov		
Heading	60 Division 179 Brigade 2/14 London Regt (London Scottish) 1915 Jan-1916 Jan		
War Diary	59 Buckingham Gate London S W	01/01/1915	21/01/1915
War Diary	Epsom Downs	22/01/1915	25/01/1915
War Diary	59 Buckingham Gate London S W	01/01/1915	21/01/1915
War Diary	Epsom Downs	22/01/1915	25/01/1915
War Diary	Reigate	26/01/1915	03/02/1915
War Diary	Reigate	26/01/1915	08/02/1915
War Diary	In Billets	09/02/1915	09/02/1915
War Diary	Denbies Park	10/02/1915	10/02/1915
War Diary	Headley Heath	11/02/1915	11/02/1915
War Diary	Neighbourhood Of Leigh	12/02/1915	12/02/1915
War Diary	Denbies Park	13/02/1915	14/02/1915
War Diary	Headley Heath	15/02/1915	15/02/1915
War Diary	Sandwich Dorking	16/02/1915	20/02/1915
War Diary	Reigate	01/02/1915	08/02/1915
War Diary	In Billets	09/02/1915	09/02/1915
War Diary	Denbies Park	10/02/1915	10/02/1915
War Diary	Headley Heath	11/02/1915	11/02/1915
War Diary	Neighbourhood Of Leigh	12/02/1915	12/02/1915
War Diary	Denbies Park	13/02/1915	14/02/1915
War Diary	Headley Heath	15/02/1915	15/02/1915
War Diary	Sandwich Dorking	16/02/1915	20/02/1915
War Diary	Reigate	01/02/1915	08/02/1915
War Diary	In Billets	09/02/1915	09/02/1915
War Diary	Denbies Park	10/02/1915	10/02/1915
War Diary	Headley Heath	11/02/1915	11/02/1915
War Diary	Neighbourhood Of Leigh	12/02/1915	12/02/1915
War Diary	Denbies Park	13/02/1915	14/02/1915
War Diary	Headley Heath	15/02/1915	15/02/1915
War Diary	Sandwich Dorking	16/02/1915	22/02/1915
War Diary	London Sandwich	23/02/1915	01/03/1915
War Diary	Dorking	20/02/1915	22/02/1915
War Diary	London Sandwich	23/02/1915	01/03/1915
War Diary	Doking	20/02/1915	22/02/1915
War Diary	London Sandwich	23/02/1915	03/03/1915
War Diary	Dorking	04/03/1915	29/03/1915
War Diary	Watford	30/03/1915	30/04/1915
War Diary	Saffron Walden	01/06/1915	04/10/1915
War Diary		01/10/1915	31/10/1915
War Diary	Bps Stortford	11/11/1915	30/11/1915
Heading	War Diary Of The 2/14th Battalion, London Regiment, (London Scottish) From 1st December 1915, To 31st, December 1915.		
War Diary	Bishops' Stortford	01/12/1915	31/12/1915
Miscellaneous	Appendix A 179th Infantry Brigade.	04/12/1915	04/12/1915
War Diary	Bishop's Stortford	01/01/1916	22/01/1916

War Diary	Sutton Veny	22/01/1916	31/01/1916
Heading	War Diary Of The 2/14th Battalion London Regiment (London Scottish) From Feb. 1st 1916 To Feb 29th. 1916		
War Diary	Sutton Veny	01/02/1916	29/02/1916
Heading	War Diary Of 2/14th Battalion London Regiment (London Scottish) From 1st March 1916 To 31st March 1916 Volume		
War Diary	Sutton Veny	01/03/1916	31/03/1916
Heading	War Diary Of The 2/14th Battalion London Regt London Scottish 1st April 1916 To 30th April 1916		
War Diary	Sutton Veny	01/04/1916	24/04/1916
War Diary	Longbridge Deverill	25/04/1916	30/04/1916
War Diary	Sutton Veny	23/04/1916	24/04/1916
War Diary	Longbridge Deverill	25/04/1916	30/04/1916
Heading	War Diary Of The 2/14th Bn London Regt. London Scottish 1st May 1916 To 31st May 1916		
War Diary	Longbridge Deverill	01/05/1916	31/05/1916
Heading	War Diary Of The 2/14th Bn London Regt London Scottish From 1st June 1916 To 20th June 1916		
War Diary	Longbridge Deverill	01/06/1916	21/06/1916
War Diary	Southampton	21/06/1916	21/06/1916
War Diary	Havre	22/06/1916	23/06/1916
War Diary	Buneville	23/06/1916	24/06/1916
War Diary	Averdoingt	25/06/1916	25/06/1916
War Diary	Maroeuil	26/06/1916	30/06/1916
Heading	War Diary Of 2/14th Bn London Regt. (London Scottish) From 1/7/16 To 31/7/16 Volume No X		
War Diary	Maroeuil	01/07/1917	05/07/1917
War Diary	Ecoivres	06/07/1917	06/07/1917
War Diary	Trenches	07/07/1917	13/07/1917
War Diary	In Trenches	14/07/1916	31/07/1916
Heading	2nd London Scottish July 16		
Map	Map		
Heading	2nd London Scottish July 16		
Heading	War Diary Of 2/14th Bn. London Regt. (London Scottish) From 1/8/16 To 31/8/16 Vol III		
War Diary	Bray	01/08/1916	31/08/1916
Heading	War Diary Of 2/14th Bn. London Regt. (London Scottish) From 1/9/16 To 30/9/16 Vol 4		
War Diary		01/09/1916	30/09/1916
Heading	War Diary Of 2/14th Battn. London Regiment From 1st October 1916-To 31st October 1916 Vol 5		
War Diary		01/10/1916	31/10/1916
Heading	2/14th Battalion London Regt (London Scottish) War Diary November 1st 1916 Vol 6		
War Diary	Montigny	01/11/1916	03/11/1916
War Diary	Buigny	04/11/1916	22/11/1916
War Diary	At Sea	23/11/1916	28/11/1916
War Diary	Salonika	29/11/1916	30/11/1916

WO 95/3030/4

60TH DIVISION
179TH INFY BDE

2-14TH BN LONDON REGT
~~JLY - NOV 1916~~

1915 JAN — 1916 NOV

60 DIVISION

179 BRIGADE

2/14 LONDON REGT
(LONDON SCOTTISH)

1915 JAN — 1916 JUN

2902

"CONFIDENTIAL"

WAR DIARY
or
INTELLIGENCE SUMMARY.
(Erase heading not required.)

Army Form C. 2118.

2/14 London

Conf 27.

Hour, Date, Place	Summary of Events and Information	Remarks and references to Appendices
59 Buckingham Gate, London, S.W.		
Jany. 1st. 1915.		
" 2nd.	Preparations for move of Battalion to Dorking.	
Jany. 4th.	Move of Battalion to Dorking.	
" 5th.	Settling down in billets. Company training.	
" 6th.	Route march and tactical exercise. Ten miles.	
" 7th.	Battalion drill and company training.	
" 8th.	Battalion drill. Company drill in extended order. x	x On the average troops 6 hours under arms.
" 9th. 11 a.m.	Inspection by Brigadier.	
2-30 p.m.	Route march 8 miles.	
" 11th.	Platoon drill started. Extended order drill. x	
" 12th.	Inspection by G.O.C. Central Force.	
" 13th.	Company training. x	
" 14th.	Route march, fourteen miles.	θ 200 packs only available.
" 15th.	Company training.	
" 16th.	" "	
" 18th.	Route march, sixteen miles.	
" 19th.	Company training. The attack. x	
" 20th.	" "	
" 21st.	Battalion and company drill. x	
" 22nd.	Inspection by Secretary of State for War.	
" 23rd. Epsom Downs.	Route march Epsom Downs to Dorking. Defence. Model entrenchments in snow.	
" 25th.	Route march via Leatherhead—thirteen miles—Advance guard formations—Attack.	

Army Form C. 2118.

THE 14TH (RESERVE) (COUNTY OF LONDON) BN.
THE LONDON REGT. (LONDON SCOTTISH)

"CONFIDENTIAL."

WAR DIARY
or
INTELLIGENCE SUMMARY.

(*Erase heading not required.*)

Instructions regarding War Diaries and Intelligence Summaries are contained in F.S. Regs., Part II. and the Staff Manual respectively. Title pages will be prepared in manuscript.

Hour, Date, Place	Summary of Events and Information	Remarks and references to Appendices
5 Buckingham Gate, London, S.W.		
Jany. 1st. 1915.	Preparations for move of Battalion to Dorking.	
" 2nd.	"	
Jany. 4th.	Move of Battalion to Dorking.	
" 5th.	Settling down in billets. Company training.	
" 6th.	Route march and tactical exercise. Ten miles. ⊘	
" 7th.	Battalion and company training. ✗	
" 8th.	Battalion drill. Company drill in extended order. ✗	
" 9th. 11 a.m.	Inspection by Brigadier.	✗ On the average troops 6 hours under arms.
2-30 p.m.	Route march 8 miles. ⊘	
" 11th.	Platoon drill started. Extended order drill. ✗	
" 12th.	Inspection by G.O.C. Central Force.	
" 13th.	Company training. ✗	
" 14th.	Route march. fourteen miles. ⊘	⊘ 200 packs only available
" 15th.	Company training. ✗	
" 16th.	"	
" 18th.	Route march. sixteen miles. ⊘	
" 19th.	Company training. The attack. ✗	
" 20th.	"	
" 21st.	Battalion and company drill. ✗	
" 22nd. Epsom Downs.	Inspection by Secretary of State for War. ⊘	
	Route march Epsom Downs to Dorking.	
	Defence. Model entrenchments in snow.	
" 23rd.	Route march via Leatherhead—thirteen miles—Advance guard formations—	
" 25th.	Attack.	

Army Form C. 2118.

WAR DIARY
or
INTELLIGENCE SUMMARY.
(*Erase heading not required.*)

Instructions regarding War Diaries and Intelligence Summaries are contained in F.S. Regs., Part II. and the Staff Manual respectively. Title pages will be prepared in manuscript.

Hour, Date, Place	Summary of Events and Information	Remarks and references to Appendices
Jany.26th.1915.(Reigate.)	Battalion and company training.	
" 27th. "	Entrenching–left Dorking 8-20 a.m.(train.) returned 5 p.m.	
" 28th. "	" " " " "	
" 29th. "	" " " " "	
" 30th. "	" " " " "	Orders to suspend all ordinary training and entrench with all Officers and men available for a fortnight.
Feb. 1st. "	" " " " "	
" 2nd. "	" " " " "	
" 3rd. "	" " " " "	

Cmmdg. A.W.Ogew.
Lt.Colonel.

THE 14TH (RESERVED) COUNTY OF LONDON BN.
THE LONDON REGT. (LONDON SCOTTISH.)

Army Form C. 2118.

WAR DIARY
or
INTELLIGENCE SUMMARY.
(Erase heading not required.)

Instructions regarding War Diaries and Intelligence Summaries are contained in F.S.Regs., Part II. and the Staff Manual respectively. Title pages will be prepared in manuscript.

4th LDN. (E.) INF. BDE.
2nd LDN. (E.) TERR DIVN.
DORKING.
FEB 4 1915
Rec. No. ....

Hour, Date, Place	Summary of Events and Information	Remarks and references to Appendices
Jany. 26th. 1915.	Battalion and company training.	
" 27th.(Reigate.)	Entrenching—left Dorking 8-20 a.m.(train.) returned 5 p.m.	
" 28th.	" " "	
" 29th.	" " "	
" 30th.	" " "	Orders to suspend all ordinary training and entrench with all Officers and men available for a fortnight.
Feb. 1st.	" " "	
" 2nd.	" " "	
" 3rd.	" " "	

A W Cogan
Lt.Colonel.
Cmmdg.
THE 14TH (RESERVED) (COUNTY OF LONDON) BN.
THE LONDON REGT. (LONDON SCOTTISH.)

2/14th Bn. LONDON REGT.
(LONDON SCOTTISH)

Army Form C. 2118.

"CONFIDENTIAL."

WAR DIARY
or
INTELLIGENCE SUMMARY.
(Erase heading not required.)

Instructions regarding War Diaries and Intelligence Summaries are contained in F. S. Regs., Part II and the Staff Manual respectively. Title pages will be prepared in manuscript.

Hour, Date, Place	Summary of Events and Information	Remarks and references to Appendices
Febry. 1st. Reigate.	Entrenching.	
" 2nd. "	"	
" 3rd. "	"	
" 4th. "	"	
" 5th. "	"	
" 6th. "	"	
" 7th. Reigate.	Sunday.	
" 8th. "	Entrenching. Issue of equipment and Japanese rifles.	
" 9th. In billets.	Cleaning billets. Kit inspection.	
" 10th. Denbies Park.	Battalion training.	
" 11th. Headley Heath.	Route march and practise of attack by companies.	
" 12th. Neighbourhood of Leigh.	Battalion tactical exercise. Brigade supervision. Order to detail 10 officers and 400 other ranks to proceed to Sandwich for Musketry on the 15th.	
" 13th. Denbies Park.	Company training.	
" 14th. ---	Sunday.	
" 15th. Headley Heath	Route march-Companies in attack with tactical objective. 10 Officers and 400 other ranks despatched to Sandwich for Musketry. Order to detail one Major and four Captains to proceed to France. Names wired G.O.C. 2/2nd. London Division.	
" 16th. Sandwich.	Musketry.	
" 17th. Dorking.	Company training.	
" 17th. Sandwich.	Musketry.	
" Dorking.	Lecture, Congregational Hall. Scrubbing out billets. Kit inspection. Lectures by Company Officers. Major and four Captains (above) ordered to proceed to Southampton.	
" 18th. Sandwich.	Musketry.	
" Dorking.	Company training.	
" 19th. Sandwich.	Musketry.	
" Dorking.	Company training. Case of Cerebro Spinal Menengitis reported in detachment at Sandwich.	
" 20th. Sandwich.	Musketry.	

(73989) W4141—463. 400,000. 9/14. H.&J.Ltd. Forms/C. 2118/10.

"CONFIDENTIAL."

2/14th Bn. LONDON REGT.
(LONDON SCOTTISH)

Army Form C. 2118.

WAR DIARY
or
INTELLIGENCE SUMMARY.
(Erase heading not required.)

Instructions regarding War Diaries and Intelligence Summaries are contained in F.S. Regs., Part II. and the Staff Manual respectively. Title pages will be prepared in manuscript.

Hour, Date, Place.	Summary of Events and Information	Remarks and references to Appendices
Febry. 1st. Reigate.	Entrenching.	
" 2nd. "	"	
" 3rd. "	"	
" 4th. "	"	
" 5th. "	"	
" 6th. "	"	
" 7th. "	Sunday.	
" 8th. Reigate.	Entrenching.	
" 9th. In billets.	Cleaning billets- Issue of equipment and Japanese rifles. Kit inspection.	
" 10th. Denbies Park.	Battalion training.	
" 11th. Headley Heath.	Route march and practise of attack by companies.	
" 12th. Neighbourhood of Leigh.	Battalion tactical exercise. Brigade supervision. Order to detail 10 officers and 400 other ranks to proceed to Sandwich for Musketry on the 15th.	
" 13th. Denbies Park.	Company training.	
" 14th. "	Sunday.	
" 15th. Headley Heath	Route march-Companies in attack with tactical objective. 10 officers and 400 other ranks despatched to Sandwich for Musketry. Order to detail one Major and four Captains to proceed to France. Names wired G.O.C. 2/2nd London Division.	
" 16th. Sandwich.	Musketry.	
" 17th. Dorking.	Company training.	
" Sandwich.	Musketry.	
" Dorking.	Lecture, Congregational Hall. Scrubbing out billets. Kit inspection. Lectures by Company Officers. Major and four Captains (above) ordered to proceed to Southampton.	
" 18th. Sandwich.	Musketry.	
" Dorking.	Company training.	
" 19th. Sandwich.	Musketry.	
" Dorking.	Company training. Case of Cerebro Spinal Meneongitis reported in detachment at Sandwich.	

"CONFIDENTIAL."

2/14th Bn. LONDON REGT.
LONDON SCOTTISH

Army Form C. 2118.

Instructions regarding War Diaries and Intelligence Summaries are contained in F.S. Regs., Part II. and the Staff Manual respectively. Title pages will be prepared in manuscript.

WAR DIARY
or
INTELLIGENCE SUMMARY.

(Erase heading not required.)

Hour, Date, Place		Summary of Events and Information	Remarks and references to Appendices
Febry.	1st. Reigate.	Entrenching.	
"	2nd. "	"	
"	3rd. "	"	
"	4th. "	"	
"	5th. "	"	
"	6th. "	"	
"	7th. - " -	- " -	
"	8th. Reigate.	Sunday.	
"	9th. In billets.	Entrenching. Cleaning billets- Issue of equipment and Japanese rifles. Kit inspection.	
"	10th. Denbies Park.	Battalion training.	
"	11th. Bendley Heath.	Route march and practise of attack by companies.	
"	12th. Neighbourhood of Leigh.	Battalion tactical exercise. Brigade supervision. Order to detail 10 officers and 400 other ranks to proceed to Sandwich for Musketry on the 15th.	
"	13th. Denbies Park.	Company training.	
"	14th. - " -	Sunday.	
"	15th. Headley Heath	Route march-Companies in attack with tactical objective. 10 Officers and 400 other ranks despatched to Sandwich for Musketry. Order to detail one Major and four Captains to proceed to France. Names wired G.O.C. 2/2nd.London Division.	
"	16th. Sandwich.	Musketry.	
"	" Dorking.	Company training.	
"	17th. Sandwich.	Musketry.	
"	" Dorking.	Lecture, Congregational Hall. Scrubbing out billets. Kit inspection. Lectures by Company Officers. Major and four Captains (above) ordered to proceed to Southampton.	
"	18th. Sandwich.	Musketry.	
"	" Dorking.	Company training.	
"	19th. Sandwich.	Musketry.	
"	" Dorking.	Company training. Case of Cerebro Spinal Meningitis reported in detachment at Sandwich.	

"CONFIDENTIAL"

Army Form C. 2118.

WAR DIARY
or
INTELLIGENCE SUMMARY.
(Erase heading not required.)

Instructions regarding War Diaries and Intelligence Summaries are contained in F.S. Regs., Part II. and the Staff Manual respectively. Title pages will be prepared in manuscript.

Hour, Date, Place	Summary of Events and Information	Remarks and references to Appendices
Febry. 20th. Dorking.	Lectures on and practice of protection. Musketry classes for N.C.O's and Privates.	
" 21st.	Owing to isolation, Sandwich, detachment officers and other ranks there not immediately available for draft called for for 1st.Battn. Order to prepare the 128 other ranks reported available Dorking for despatch overseas as rapidly as possible and detail Conducting Officer.	
" 22nd.	Move of Battalion (less Sandwich Draft, necessary details, sick and isolated men) to London. March Victoria - Hyde Park. Drill in Hyde Park - March to Provisional Headquarters, Wesleyan Hall Westminster. Men less some 20 billeted in neighbourhood allowed to go home for night.	
" 23rd. London. Sandwich.	Route march - Musketry squads. Detachment less some 40 men isolated, moved to London. Dorking- Details.	
" 24th.	As on 23rd.	
" 25th.	As on 23rd.	
	Conducting Officer and 128 other ranks from Dorking plus 290 non contact other ranks from Sandwich reported ready to move overseas Saturday. Strength Officers, other ranks, horses, weight of baggage for move of Battalion less Draft back from London to Dorking wired Divisional Headquarters, Reigate.	
" 26th.	As on 23rd. - G.O.C. 2/2nd. London Division to inspect Draft at 59 Buckingham Gate on 27th. Draft to accompany Battalion to Dorking.	
" 27th.b	Route march - Draft inspected as above at 2pm. Application made for draft of 300 other ranks to be sent to 2/14th. from 3/14th.Battalion. Order that Officers and other ranks Draft to remain in London and not to go to Dorking with Battalion.	
" 28th.	Names of 3 additional Conducting Officers for Draft sent in. Return of Battalion less Draft and men isolated at Sandwich to Dorking.	
March. 1st.	Swedish drill - Company training - Musketry squads.	

"CONFIDENTIAL"

Army Form C. 2118.

WAR DIARY
or
INTELLIGENCE SUMMARY.
(Erase heading not required.)

Instructions regarding War Diaries and Intelligence Summaries are contained in F.S. Regs., Part II and the Staff Manual respectively. Title pages will be prepared in manuscript.

Hour, Date, Place	Summary of Events and Information	Remarks and references to Appendices
Febry. 20th. Dorking.	Lectures on and practice of protection. Musketry classes for N.C.O's and Privates.	
" 21st.	Owing to isolation, Sandwich, detachment officers and other ranks there not immediately available for draft called for 1st. Battn. Order to prepare the 128 other ranks reported available Dorking for despatch overseas as rapidly as possible and detail Conducting Officer.	
" 22nd.	Move of Battalion (less Sandwich Draft, necessary details, sick and isolated men) to London. March Victoria - Hyde Park - Drill in Hyde Park - March to Provisional Headquarters, Wesleyan Hall Westminster. Men less some 20 billeted in neighbourhood allowed to go home for night. Route march. - Musketry squads. Detachment less some 40 men isolated, moved to London. Dorking- Details.	
" 23rd. London.	As on 23rd.	
" 24th. Sandwich.	As on 23rd.	
" 25th.	Conducting Officer and 128 other ranks from Dorking plus 290 non contact other ranks from Sandwich reported ready to move overseas Saturday. Strength Officers, other ranks, horses, weight of baggage for move of Battalion less Draft back from London to Dorking wired Divisional Headquarters, Reigate.	
" 26th.	As on 23rd. - G.O.C. 2/2nd. London Division to inspect Draft at 59 Buckingham Gate on 27th. Draft to accompany Battalion to Dorking.	
" 27th.b	Route march. - Draft inspected as above at 2pm. Application made for draft of 300 other ranks to be sent to 2/14th. from 3/14th. Battalion. Order that Officers and other ranks Draft to remain in London and not to go to Dorking with Battalion.	
" 28th.	Names of 3 additional Conducting Officers for Draft sent in. Return of Battalion less Draft and men isolated at Sandwich to Dorking.	
March.1st.	Swedish drill - Company training - Musketry squads.	

Army Form C. 2118.

WAR DIARY
or
INTELLIGENCE SUMMARY.
(Erase heading not required.)

Hour, Date, Place	Summary of Events and Information	Remarks and references to Appendices
Febry.20th.Dorking.		
" 21st.	Lectures on and practice of protection. Musketry classes for N.C.O's and Privates.	
" 22nd.	Owing to isolation,Sandwich,detachment officers and other ranks there not immediately available for draft called for for 1st.Battn. Order to prepare the 128 other ranks reported available Dorking for despatch overseas as rapidly as possible and detail Conducting Officer. Move of Battalion (less Sandwich Draft,necessary details,sick and isolated men) to London.	
" 23rd. London.	March Victoria - Hyde Park - Drill in Hyde Park - March to Provisional Headquarters, Wesleyan Hall Westminster. Men less some 20 billeted in neighbourhood allowed to go home for night. Route march - Musketry Squads.	
" 24th. Sandwich.	Detachment less some 40 men isolated, moved to London.Dorking- Details.	
" 25th.	As on 23rd.	
	As on 23rd. Conducting Officer and 128 other ranks from Dorking plus 290 non contact other ranks from Sandwich reported ready to move overseas Saturday. Strength Officers,other ranks,horses,weight of baggage for move of Battalion less Draft back from London to Dorking wired Divisional Headquarters,Reigate.	
" 26th.	As on 23rd. - G.O.C. 2/2nd.London Division to inspect Draft at 59 Buckingham Gate on 27th.Draft to accompany Battalion to Dorking.	
" 27th.5	Route march - Draft inspected as above at 2pm. Application made for draft of 300 other ranks to be sent to 2/14th. from 3/14th.Battalion. Order that Officers and other ranks Draft to remain in London and not to go to Dorking with Battalion. Names of 3 additional Conducting Officers for Draft sent in.	
" 28th.	Return of Battalion less Draft and men isolated at Sandwich to Dorking.	
March.1st.	Swedish drill - Company training - Musketry squads.	

"CONFIDENTIAL"

Army Form C. 2118.

Instructions regarding War Diaries and Intelligence Summaries are contained in F.S. Regs., Part II. and the Staff Manual respectively. Title pages will be prepared in manuscript.

WAR DIARY
or
INTELLIGENCE SUMMARY.
(Erase heading not required.)

Hour, Date, Place	Summary of Events and Information	Remarks and references to Appendices
March.2nd.	Authorisation to give 48 hours leave to other ranks Draft. Order that Draft to be ready to march on 5th. Leave given until 8 p.m. on 4th. - Route march, Companies in attack - Names of three additional Officers to proceed to France wired Divisional Headquarters.	
" 3rd.	Order that four Conducting Officers detailed for Draft and the 398 other ranks to report Peace Headquarters, London Scottish for duty by 8pm.March 4th. Lecture on outposts - Practice of outposts.	

A.W.Orgee.
Lt.Colonel.
Cmndg.
2/14th Bn. LONDON REGT.
(LONDON SCOTTISH)

WAR DIARY or INTELLIGENCE SUMMARY

Army Form C. 2118.

Hour, Date, Place	Summary of Events and Information	Remarks and references to Appendices
March 2nd.	Authorisation to give 48 hours leave to other ranks Draft. Order that Draft to be ready to march on 5th. Leave given until 8 p.m. on 4th. - Route march. Companies in attack - Names of three additional Officers to proceed to France wired Divisional Headquarters.	
" 3rd.	Order that four Conducting Officers detailed for Draft and the 398 other ranks to report Peace Headquarters, London Scottish for duty by 8p.m.March 4th. Lecture on outposts - Practice of outposts.	

A.W.Coupe.
Lt.Colonel.
Cmdg.
2/14th Bn. LONDON REGT.
(LONDON SCOTTISH)

"CONFIDENTIAL"

Army Form C. 2118.

Instructions regarding War Diaries and Intelligence
Summaries are contained in F.S. Regs., Part II.
and the Staff Manual respectively. Title pages
will be prepared in manuscript.

WAR DIARY
or
INTELLIGENCE SUMMARY.
(Erase heading not required.)

Hour, Date, Place	Summary of Events and Information	Remarks and references to Appendices
March.2nd.	Authorisation to give 48 hours leave to other ranks Draft. Order that Draft to be ready to march on 5th. Leave given until 8 pm. on 4th. - Route march, Companies in attack - Names of three additional Officers to proceed to France wired Divisional Headquarters.	
" 3rd.	Order that four Conducting Officers detailed for Draft and the 398 other ranks to report Peace Headquarters, London Scottish for duty by 8pm.March 4th. Lecture on outposts - Practice of outposts.	

A W Doyer?
Lt. Colonel.
Cmndg.
2/14th Bn. LONDON REGT.
(LONDON SCOTTISH.)

Army Form C. 2118.

WAR DIARY
or
INTELLIGENCE SUMMARY.
(Erase heading not required.)

Instructions regarding War Diaries and Intelligence Summaries are contained in F.S. Regs., Part II. and the Staff Manual respectively. Title pages will be prepared in manuscript.

Hour, Date, Place	Summary of Events and Information	Remarks and references to Appendices
March 4th. Dorking.	Company training.	
" 5th.	Brigade outpost Scheme.- Instructions received by telephone for draft to be split up. 130 to receive fresh warning orders and remainder to have time of departure notified later. Telegram from London District instructing Lt.Newington, 2nd.Lt. W.H.Anderson, and 2nd.Lt.C.P.Roberson to proceed to Southampton.	
" 6th.	Physical drill.- Company training - Kit inspection. Telegram from Sea Rail ordering 1 Officer and 130 other ranks to proceed to Southampton.	
" 7th.	1 Officer and 130 other ranks proceeded to Southampton. Telegram received from 2/2nd.London Division ordering remainder of draft to remain in London.	
" 8th.	Physical drill. - Musketry - Bayonet fighting. Battalion drill. 289 N.C.Os and Men joined from 3/14th.Battalion.	
" 9th.	Physical drill. Musketry. Extended order.	
" 10th.	Physical drill. Company and Battalion drill.	
" 11th.	Physical drill. Extended order and attack practice.	
	Recruits drill. Musketry. Lecture by the M.O.	
" 12th.	Brigade training in the attack.	
	Capt.G.M.Ford returned to duty on expiration of sick leave.	
" 13th.	Physical drill. Company training. Kit inspection.	
" 15th.	Physical drill. Company training.	
" 16th.	Physical drill. Company training. Extended order.	
" 17th.	Physical drill. Training in protection. Musketry.	
xxx14thxxxxxx	Draft of 3 conducting Officers and 253 N.C.Os and Men proceeded to Southampton.	
" 18th.	Physical drill. Company training in attack. Musketry. Capt.J.H.Lindsey joined on termination of appointment as Staff Captain 1/4th.London Infantry Brigade, and was appointed Acting Major.	
" 19th.	Route March.	
" 20th.	Physical drill.- Company training. Officers revolver course.	

(73989) W4141--463. 400,000. 9/14. H.&J.Ltd. Forms/C. 2118/10.

Army Form C. 2118.

WAR DIARY
or
INTELLIGENCE SUMMARY.
(Erase heading not required.)

Instructions regarding War Diaries and Intelligence Summaries are contained in F.S. Regs., Part II. and the Staff Manual respectively. Title pages will be prepared in manuscript.

Hour, Date, Place		Summary of Events and Information	Remarks and references to Appendices
March. 21st.	Dorking.	2nd.Lt.H.C.Sparkes name forwarded to Usted in response to telegram.	
" 22nd.	"	Brigade tactical Scheme. Telegram from Usted instructing 2nd.Lt. H.C.Sparkes to proceed to join 1/14th.Battn. at once. Complied with.	
" 23rd.	"	Physical drill.- Company and Battalion drill.	
" 24th.	"	Physical drill.- Extended order.- Musketry.	
" 25th.	"	Company concentration march.	
" 26th.	"	Physical drill.Musketry. Battalion training in attack.	
" 27th.	"	Physical Drill.Musketry. Company training.	
" 29th.	"	Battalion moved to Watford.	
" 30th.	Watford.	Physical Drill.Bayonet Exercise.Musketry. Coy. and Battn. drill.	
" 31st.	"	Battalion March. advanced and Rear Guards.	

(73989) W4141—463. 400,000. 9/14. H.&J.Ltd. Forms/C. 2118/10.

Draft of
WAR DIARY
or
INTELLIGENCE SUMMARY.
(Erase heading not required.)

Army Form C. 2118.

Instructions regarding War Diaries and Intelligence Summaries are contained in F.S. Regs., Part II. and the Staff Manual respectively. Title pages will be prepared in manuscript.

Hour, Date, Place	Summary of Events and Information	Remarks and references to Appendices
Watford. 1/4/15.	Physical Drill, Battalion Exercise and Battalion attack in Grove Park.	
2/4/15.	Good Friday - Church Parade for Church of England men.	
3/4/15.	Kit Inspection & Trial Alarm.	
4/4/15.	Sunday - Church Parade.	
5/4/15.	Easter Monday - Bank Holiday for troops.	
6/4/15.	Brigade Concentration March.	
7/4/15.	Coy. & Battalion Training in Close Order. Cassiobury Park.	
8/4/15.	Coy. Attack & Defence.	
	Divisional Headquarters telephoned giving copy of Third Army Telegram, requesting us to wire Timoleon & Central Force as to the numbers available for an immediate draft.	
9/4/15.	Battalion Concentration March to Leverstock Green.	
	Proposed Draft examined by Medical Officer and Telegram sent to Timoleon, Central Force & Third Army advising a draft available of 102 other ranks.	
	Application forwarded to Headquarters 2/4th London Infantry Brigade to bring 2/14th Battalion up to strength.	
10/4/15. Sat.		
11/4/15.	Sunday - Church Parade.	
	Divisional Headquarters telephoned to "Expedite all clothing and equipment of 102 other ranks.	

Army Form C. 2118.

WAR DIARY
or
INTELLIGENCE SUMMARY.
(Erase heading not required.)

Instructions regarding War Diaries and Intelligence Summaries are contained in F.S. Regs., Part II. and the Staff Manual respectively. Title pages will be prepared in manuscript.

Hour, Date, Place	Summary of Events and Information	Remarks and references to Appendices
12/4/15.	Telephone message from Divisional Headquarters received to the effect than an officer is required to conduct reinforcements of 1/14th Bn. Name to be sent on to Division at once.	
	Confirmation of telephone message of the 11th inst. to expedite draft received.	
	Our Reg. Letter No. 1554 sent to H.Q. 2/2nd London Div. recommending 2nd Lt. G. F. T. Horne for conducting duty.	
13/4/15.	Telephone message from Divisional Headquarters received giving copy of Third Army Telegram A.Q.61. calling for reports as to the draft in preparation and the date it will be ready to move.	
	Our Reg. Telegram No 93. forwarded to Timoleon, Central Force, Third Army & H.Q. 2/2nd London Division, stating that the draft would probably be ready for inspection on the afternoon of the 16/4/15.	
	Advice sent to Sec. T.F.A. that a draft of 102 other ranks had been ordered.	
	Our Reg. Letter No. 1578 forwarded to O.C. Records applying for a draft of 219 other ranks to bring the strength of this Battalion up to Establishment.	
	Nominal Roll of Draft of 102 other ranks forwarded to Record Office to be checked	in accordance with W.O.Letter 121/1720 (A.G.2a) dated 1/2/15
14/4/15.	Telegram Reg. No. 94 forwarded to Timoleon & Central Force,/advising remaining strength of Battalion as follows:- 8 Trained men and 672 Recruits, Military Station St.Albans & Watford, Nearest Station Watford Junction, and that draft would be ready for inspection on Friday 16/4/15.	
	Picquet posted at the Three Bridges in accordance with Secret Instructions.	

Army Form C. 2118.

WAR DIARY
or
INTELLIGENCE SUMMARY.
(Erase heading not required.)

Instructions regarding War Diaries and Intelligence Summaries are contained in F.S. Regs., Part II and the Staff Manual respectively. Title pages will be prepared in manuscript.

Hour, Date, Place	Summary of Events and Information	Remarks and references to Appendices
14/4/15.	Telegram received in Orderly Room from Centreforce. Reg. No. C12442 detailing 2nd Lt. G. F. T. Horne to conduct the draft across to 1/14th Bn.	
15/4/15.	Telegram received from Medical Board, Caxton Hall, advising 2nd Lt. C. Cornock Taylor found fit for Light Home Duty. Telegram received from O.C. 3/14th Battn. asking for the services of 2nd Lt. Cornock-Taylor. Reply sent "Have no authority to grant the necessary permission". Picquets posted as on 14/4/15.	
16/4/15.	Concentration March by the Battalion at Bovingdon. Picquets posted as on the May 14-15/4/15.	
17/4/15.	Our Reg. Telegram No. 98 forwarded to Timoleon stating that draft would be ready to move at 3 p.m. 20/4/15, and that letter had been received from O.C. Records stating all all 1/14th men with the 3/14th Battn. found fit, were to join our draft.	O.C. Records that all 1/14th men found fit are to join the draft.
	Confirmation of Telegram received through Brigade Headquarters that 2nd Lt. G. F. T. Horne has been detailed to conduct the draft to overseas base.	
18/4/15.	Sunday - Church Parade. Telegram telephoned to us by Divisional Headquarters from the Third Army Reg. No. A.C.73 calling for further draft of 38 other ranks.	
19/4/15.	Telegram No. A.1046 C.M.G. 2 giving instructions for draft to proceed from Watford to Southampton received from Seaforth.	
20/4/15.	Letter received from O.C. 3/14th Bn. stating that the 1/14th men were being sent down on the 21/4/15. Telegram forwarded to Timoleon, Centreforce & Third army our Reg. No. 101, advising 8 available other ranks, and that we understand 3/14th Battn. has 26.	

Army Form C. 2118.

WAR DIARY
or
INTELLIGENCE SUMMARY.
(Erase heading not required.)

Instructions regarding War Diaries and Intelligence Summaries are contained in F.S. Regs., Part II and the Staff Manual respectively. Title pages will be prepared in manuscript.

Hour, Date, Place	Summary of Events and Information	Remarks and references to Appendices
21/4/15.		
22/4/15.		
23/4/15.	~~Confirmation~~ Telegram received through Brigade Headquarters that the number of draft required is 34.	
24/4/15.	~~Third Army Telegram A.Q. 96 received~~	
25/4/15.	Third Army Telegram A.Q. 96 received through Brigade Headquarters, detailing 2nd Lt. H. M. Clowes to conduct draft of 34 other ranks to oversees base.	
26/4/15.	Tactical Scheme. No. 1712	
27/4/15.	Letter/forwarded to Sec. T.F.A. advising a further draft of 34 ordered. Letter No. 1715 forwarded to O.C. Records giving list of proposed draft. Divisional Headquarters telephoned giving copy of Third Army Telegram No. A.Q.104 instructing us to expedite preparations of draft.and to forward usual reports.	
28/4/15.	Reg. Telegram No. 109 forwarded to Tincleon, Central Force & Third Army stating draft would be ready to move immediately after inspection by G.O.C. on morning of 29/4/15.	
29/4/15.	Draft inspected by Col. E. D. Baird Comdg. 2/4th London Infantry Brigade on Battalion alarm Post at 3 p.m.	
30/4/15.	Brigade Exercise.	

Army Form C. 2118.

WAR DIARY
or
INTELLIGENCE SUMMARY.
(Erase heading not required.)

Instructions regarding War Diaries and Intelligence Summaries are contained in F.S. Regs., Part II. and the Staff Manual respectively. Title pages will be prepared in manuscript.

Hour, Date, Place	Summary of Events and Information	Remarks and references to Appendices
Saffron Walden. Tues. 1st. June.1915.	Company and Battalion training in close order drill in Shortgrove Park in accordance with Brigade Programme.	
Wed. 2nd. "	Occupation of a village.Defence and Administration,as per Brigade Programme.	
Thurs.3rd. "	Morning. Companies and Battalion in close order drill,Grass Park. Night. Battalion marching by night in accordance with Brigade programme.	
Fri. 4th. "	Outpost scheme by Battalion in Audley End Park.	
Sat. 5th. "	Company drill and Kit inspection, Shortgrove Park,as per Brigade programme.	
Sun. 6th. "	Divine Service.	
Mon. 7th. "	Brigade night work.Training as per Brigade Programme.	
Tues. 8th. "	Company and Battalion training in Debden Park as per Brigade programme.	
Wed. 9th. "	Reconnaissance in Grass Park, as per Brigade programme.	
Thurs.10th. "	Battalion taking up positions at night, between Cloptons and Butlers Farm. Battalion training in Audley End Park in morning.	
Fri. 11th. "	Company and Battalion in attack and defence, Shortgrove Park.	
Sat. 12th. "	Kit inspection and Company drill in Debden Park.	
Sun. 13th. "	Divine Service.	
Mon. 14th. "	Brigade Scheme.	
Tues. 15th. "	Company and Battalion in close order drill, in Grass Park.	
Wed. 16th. "	Extended order drill and Ceremonial in Audley End Park.	
Thurs.17th. "	Inspection by G.O.C. Third Army.	
Fri. 18th. "	Company and Battalion training.	
Sat. 19th. "	Kit inspection and Company training in Debden Park.	
Sun. 20th. "	Divine Service.	
Mon. 21st. "	Brigade Scheme.	
Tues. 22nd. "	Company and Battalion in close order drill in Grass Park as per Brigade Programme.	
Wed. 23rd. "	Company and Battalion in close order drill in Audley End Park as per Brigade programme.	

Army Form C. 2118.

WAR DIARY
or
INTELLIGENCE SUMMARY.
(Erase heading not required.)

Instructions regarding War Diaries and Intelligence Summaries are contained in F.S. Regs., Part II. and the Staff Manual respectively. Title pages will be prepared in manuscript.

Hour, Date, Place	Summary of Events and Information	Remarks and references to Appendices
Saffron Walden.		
Wed. 23rd June 1915	(Continued.) Instructions received to prepare a draft of 210 other ranks as reinforcements to 1/14th. Bn. Draft of 18 required at once.	
Thurs. 24th. "	Company and Battalion training in close order drill in Shortgrove park as per Brigade programme. Medical inspection of draft commenced. Draft of 18 inspected by Col. E. W. Baird, Comdg 2/4th. London Infantry Brigade.	
Fri. 25th. "	Divisional Scheme. Parade strong as possible. Medical inspection postponed until Saturday.	
Sat. 26th. "	Kit inspection and Company training in Grass Park as per Brigade programme. Draft of 18 other ranks proceeded to Southampton under 2nd. Lt. J.S. Munro. Medical inspection of draft continued.	
Sun. 27th. "	Divine Service. Telephone message received from O.C. Records that all 1st. Battalion men held as supernumerary to 3/14th. Battalion to be made nucleus of draft of 192, to complete the original 210 called for. Telegram despatched to 3/14th. Battalion calling for numbers available.	
Mon. 28th. "	Draft paraded with Battalion on Brigade Scheme. pending numbers available from 3/14th. Battalion. Telegram received from 3/14th. Battn. 16 men available. Telegram despatched to O.C. Records to authorise the 16 men to be sent here to be equipped.	
Tues. 29th. "	Draft of 9 other ranks arrived from London but only 2 passed by my Medical Officer as fit. Companies and Battalion in close order drill in Grass Park in accordance with Brigade programme.	
Wed. 30th. "	Battalion and Company drill in close order drill in Shortgrove Park as per brigade programme. Draft practically complete of clothing and equipment.	

Major.
Comdg.

Army Form C. 2118.

WAR DIARY
or
INTELLIGENCE SUMMARY.
(Erase heading not required.)

Instructions regarding War Diaries and Intelligence Summaries are contained in F. S. Regs., Part II. and the Staff Manual respectively. Title pages will be prepared in manuscript.

Hour, Date, Place	Summary of Events and Information	Remarks and references to Appendices
1/7/15. Saffron Walden.	Coy. Training in Shortgrove Park. Draft of 192 other ranks inspected by Col. E.W.D.Baird, Comdg. 2/4th London Infantry Brigade and granted 48 hours leave at 4 p.m. Telegram received from SHARATH at 7 p.m. stating draft would leave Saffron Walden at 6.15 a.m. the following morning. Telegrams were immediately despatched to those N.C.O'S & men who had got away, and messages were sent to the London Railway termini by telegraph and telephone to return the men to Saffron Walden.	
2/7/15. do.	Draft of 172 other ranks left at 6.15 a.m. Musketry Party proceeded to Welwyn. Battalion practised in Escort and Defence of a Convoy.	
3/7/15. do.	Kit Inspection, etc.	
4/7/15. do.	Divine Service. The balance of draft of 20 other ranks left under 2nd Lt. G. Wallis.	
5/7/15. do.	Brigade Tactical Scheme. Night concentration march to neighbourhood of Ellis Green.	
6/7/15. do.	Battalion Drill in Debden Park.	
7/7/15. do.	Battalion Drill in Grass Park.	
8/7/15. do.	Outpost and Reconnaissance practised in Audley End Park.	
9/7/15. do.	2nd Lieuts. A.G.Duncan and A.H.Macgregor proceeded to Southampton en route to join the 1/14th Battalion. Company Drill in Shortgrove Park and Lectures. Draft of 69 other ranks arrived from 3/14th Battalion. Musketry Party returned to duty from Welwyn.	
10/7/15. do.	2nd.Lt. G.E.Godsave proceeded to Southampton en route to join the 1/14th Battn. Kit Inspection, etc.	

Army Form C. 2118.

WAR DIARY
or
INTELLIGENCE SUMMARY.
(Erase heading not required.)

Instructions regarding War Diaries and Intelligence Summaries are contained in F.S. Regs., Part II and the Staff Manual respectively. Title pages will be prepared in manuscript.

Hour, Date, Place	Summary of Events and Information	Remarks and references to Appendices
11/7/15. Saffron Walden.	Divine Service.	
12/7/15. do.	Battalion Training in Debden Park.	
13/7/15. do.	2nd Lieut. A.G.MacLean transferred to the 3/6th Bn. Gordon Hrs. as a Lieut. Company and Battalion Training in Close Order Drill in Grass Park.	
14/7/15. do.	Battalion practised in the Occupation of a village at Arkesdon.	
15/7/15. do.	Companies practised in the Attack in Audley End Park.	
16/7/15. do.	Draft of 51 1/14th Battalion men returned to the 3/14th Battalion. Draft of 31 3/14th Battalion men arrived, and taken on the strength. Lectures to Battalion on account of heavy rain.	
17/7/15. do.	Capt. E.M.Stirling proceeded to Southampton en route to join the 1/14th Battalion. Kit Inspection, etc.	
18/7/15. do.	Divine Service.	
19/7/15. do.	Battalion Training in Debden Park.	
20/7/15. do.	Company and Battalion practised in Close Order Drill in Grass Park.	
21/7/15. do.	Reconnaissance and Outposts practised in Audley End Park.	
22/7/15. do.	Company and Battalion Training in Close Order Drill in Shortgrove Park.	
23/7/15. do.	Draft of N.4 men arrived from 3/14th Battalion and taken on the strength. Usual morning work. At night, Timed Night March via Radwinter and Ashdon.	

Army Form C. 2118.

WAR DIARY
or
INTELLIGENCE SUMMARY.
(Erase heading not required.)

Instructions regarding War Diaries and Intelligence Summaries are contained in F.S. Regs., Part II. and the Staff Manual respectively. Title pages will be prepared in manuscript.

Hour, Date, Place	Summary of Events and Information	Remarks and references to Appendices
24/7/15. Saffron Walden.	Kit Inspection, etc.	
25/7/15. do.	Divine Service.	
26/7/15. do.	Draft of 26 other ranks for Home Service sent to 104th Provisional Battn. T.F. under and Lieut. D. B. Edsall. Battalion practised in taking up a defensive position in Brigade East of Arsdon.	
27/7/15. do.	Company and Battalion in Close Order Drill in Audley End Park.	
28/7/15. do.	Companies practised in the Attack in Shortgrove Park.	
29/7/15. do.	Companies and Battalion in Close Order Drill in Debden Park. Communication received through the 2/4th London Infantry Brigade that all men above a minimum strength of 600 are to be available for an immediate draft. Telegram despatched to Timoleon giving the number as 101.	
30/7/15. do.	Draft examined by Medical Officer, also clothed and equipped and granted leave until Sunday night, August 1st, 1915. Battalion usual morning training. At night, Battalion practised in taking up a position in the neighbourhood of Littlebury (Green and the Evacuation of Wounded by night.	
31/7/15. do.	Kit Inspection, etc.	

Major.
Comdg. 2/34th Battn. London Regt. (London Scottish).

WAR DIARY
or
INTELLIGENCE SUMMARY.
(Erase heading not required.)

Army Form C. 2118.

Hour, Date, Place	Summary of Events and Information	Remarks and references to Appendices
Saffron Walden. 1/8/1915.	Divine Service.	
2/8/15.	Bank H.Kay for Troops. Representatives of the Battalion attended 2/2nd London Divisional Sports at Bishops Stortford, and carried off the "Cup" for the "Marathon".	
3/8/15.	Battalion at Shortgrove Park. Lectures owing to heavy rain. Draft of 101 other ranks inspected by Col. E.W.D.Baird, Comdg. 179th Infantry Brigade, and telegram forwarded to Timoleon, Centreforce, Third Army and 2/2nd London Division to this effect, and also that the draft would be ready to move on receipt of six hours notice. Orders received to return all Home Service Officers and men to the 104th Provisional Battalion (T.F.) at once.	
4/8/15.	Battalion moved into Camp in Ferrycroft Road. Detachment trained in Entrenching by day.	
5/8/15.	Battalion at Grass Park. Close Order Drill. Entrenching at night. Maj.R.Crerar transferred to the 3/3th Bn. Middlesex Regt. as Lt.Col. 2nd.Lt.J.A.Robertson relinquished his Commission, for the purpose of entering the Royal Navy.	
6/8/15.	Battalion at Audley End Park. Entrenching by day.	
7/8/15.	Kit Inspection, Foot Inspection, etc. 2nd Lt. G.D.H.Mackinnon transferred to 104th Provisional Bn (T.F).	
8/8/15.	Divine Service.	
9/8/15.	Party detailed for North Mimms and subsequently cancelled.	
10/8/15.	Battalion at Shortgrove Park.	
11/8/15.	Musketry Party left for North Mimms. Battalion Entrenching by day. Entrenching by night.	
12/8/15.	Battalion Training in Camp.	
13/8/15.	Battalion at Audley End Park. Close Order Drill. No.4485. Pte. H.L.Lindsay killed by Motor Omnibus in London.	
13/8/15.	Entrenching by Day. Musketry Party returned from N.Mimms.	
14/8/15.	Train Orders Received for Draft. Kit & Foot Inspection, etc.	

WAR DIARY
or
INTELLIGENCE SUMMARY.
(Erase heading not required.)

Army Form C. 2118.

Hour, Date, Place		Summary of Events and Information	Remarks and references to Appendices
Saff.Walden.	14/8/15.	Capt. A.C.H.Parker Smith transferred to the 3/4th Bn. Argyll & Sutherland Highlanders as a Captain.	
	15/8/15.	Draft of 101 other ranks under 2nd Lt.N.Hunter proceeded to Southampton, en route to join the 1/14th Bn. in France. Divine Service.	
	16/8/15.	Battalion at Debden Park. Close Order Drill.	
	17/8/15.	Battalion practised in entrenching.	
	18/8/15.	Battalion practised in entrenching at Night.	
	19/8/15.	Battalion practised in Defence of a Village at Ashdon.	
	20/8/15.	One Company practised in Outposts. Remainder of Battalion entrenching by day.	
	21/8/15.	Kit & Foot Inspection, etc. 2nd Lt. G.F.T. Horne transferred to the Inns of Court O.T.C. as a 2nd Lieutenant.	
	22/8/15.	Divine Service.	
	23/8/15.	Route March.	
	24/8/15.	Battalion Outpost Scheme.	
	25/8/15.	Taking up a Defensive Position.	
	26/8/15.	Musketry Party left for North Mimms. Entrenching by Night.	
	27/8/15.	Advance Guard Action from Arkesden to Wendon.	
	28/8/15.	Kit Inspection, etc. accompanied by Col. R.L.D.Baird, Brigadier, Col. Long, Director of Mechanical Transport,/inspected Transport, of Bn.	
	29/8/15.	Divine Service.	
	30/8/15.	Battalion practised in The Attack in the neighbourhood of Hadstock.	
	31/8/15.	Battalion practised in taking up an outpost position.	

Major.
Comdg. 2/14th Bn. London Regt.
(London Scottish).

Army Form C. 2118.

WAR DIARY
or
INTELLIGENCE SUMMARY.
(Erase heading not required.)

Instructions regarding War Diaries and Intelligence Summaries are contained in F.S. Regs., Part II. and the Staff Manual respectively. Title pages will be prepared in manuscript.

Hour, Date, Place	Summary of Events and Information	Remarks and references to Appendices
Saffron Walden. 1/9/15.	Battalion practised in the Attack of a Convoy.	
2/9/15.	Entrenching by day.	
3/9/15.	Battalion practised in the Defence of Little Walden Park Farm.	
4/9/15.	Musketry party returned from N. Mimms.	
4/9/15.	Kit & Foot Inspection, etc.	
5/9/15.	Divine Service.	
6/9/15.	Defensive position taken up by Battalion.	
7/9/15.	Battalion practised in Trench Work. Lt.Col. A.E.Rogers transferred to T.F.R.	
8/9/15.	Battalion practised in the Attack of a position in Country areas. Major. R. Dunsmore appointed (Temp) Lt. Colonel.	
8/9/15.	Zeppelin seen over camp - proceeding due East.	
9/9/15.	Battalion practised in Trench Work.	
10/9/15.	Battalion Reconnaissance Scheme.	
11/9/15.	Kit & Foot Inspection, etc. 2nd Lt. W. Anderson returned from Musketry School, Bisley.	
12/9/15.	Divine Service.	
13/9/15.	Brigade Outpost Scheme and Mess Tin Cooking. Capt. G. N. Ford returned to duty from Third Army Headquarters.	
14/9/15.	179th Brigade Signal Coy. under 2nd Lt. C.Threcher, R.E. attached to Camp Duties.	
15/9/15.	Battalion for Discipline, Accommodation and Rations. Battalion practised in advance over open Country.	
16/9/15.	Battalion practised in Company Concentration by Platoons. 2nd Lt. H. H. Reid transferred to R.F.A. Lowland Brigade. 2nd Lt. D. L. Macrae returned from Perivale School of Instruction.	
17/9/15.	Night Operations.	
18/9/15.	Kit & Foot Inspection, etc.	
19/9/15.	Divine Service.	
20/9/15.	Battalion practised in Reconnaissance of a position.	

Army Form C. 2118.

WAR DIARY
or
INTELLIGENCE SUMMARY.
(Erase heading not required.)

Instructions regarding War Diaries and Intelligence Summaries are contained in F.S. Regs., Part II and the Staff Manual respectively. Title pages will be prepared in manuscript.

Hour, Date, Place	Summary of Events and Information	Remarks and references to Appendices
Saffron Walden. 1/9/15.	Battalion practised in the Attack of a Convoy.	
2/9/15.	Entrenching by day.	
3/9/15.	Battalion practised in the Defence of Little Walden Park Farm.	
4/9/15.	Musketry party returned from N. Miums.	
4/9/15.	Kit & Foot Inspection, etc.	
5/9/15.	Divine Service.	
6/9/15.	Defensiveposition taken up by Battalion.	
7/9/15.	Battalion practised in Trench Work. Lt.Col. A.E.Rogers transferred to T.P.R.	
8/9/15.	Battalion Practised in the Attack of a position in Country areas. Major. R. Dunsmore appointed (Temp) Lt. Colonel.	
9/9/15.	Zeppelin seen over camp - proceeding due East.	
9/9/15.	Battalion practised in Trench Work.	
10/9/15.	Battalion Reconnaisance Scheme.	
11/9/15.	Kit & Foot Inspection, etc. 2nd Lt. W. Anderson returned from Musketry School, Bisley.	
12/9/15.	Divine Service.	
13/9/15.	Brigade Outpost Scheme and Mess Tin Cooking. Capt. G. M. Ford returned to duty from Third Army Headquarters.	
14/9/15.	Camp Duties. 179th Brigade Signal Coy. under 2nd Lt. C.Thrasher, R.E. attached to Battalion for Discipline, Accomodation and Rations.	
15/9/15.	Battalion practised in advance over open Country.	
16/9/15.	Battalion practised in Company Concentration by Platoons. 2nd Lt. H. M. Reid transferred to R.F.A. Lowland Brigade. 2nd Lt. D. L. Macrae returned from Perivale School of Instruction.	
17/9/15.	Night Operations.	
18/9/15.	Kit & Foot Inspection, etc.	
19/9/15.	Divine Service.	
20/9/15.	Battalion practised in Reconnaissance of a position.	

WAR DIARY
or
INTELLIGENCE SUMMARY.

(Erase heading not required.)

Army Form C. 2118.

Instructions regarding War Diaries and Intelligence Summaries are contained in F. S. Regs., Part II and the Staff Manual respectively. Title pages will be prepared in manuscript.

Hour, Date, Place	Summary of Events and Information	Remarks and references to Appendices
Saffron Walden. 21/9/15.	Battalion practised in Attack & Defence. Capt. G. M. Ford attached to Divisional Headquarters for instruction under the A.A. & Q.M.G.	
22/9/15.	Route March.	
23/9/15.	Alarm Parade. Brigade Concentration at Quendon Park.	
24/9/15.	Company & Battalion in Close Order Drill.	
25/9/15.	Kit & Foot Inspection, etc.	
27/9/15.	Brigade Manoeuvres at Gt. Chishall and vicinity. 2nd Lts. F. W. Roberts and D. L. Macrae proceeded to the 1/14th Bn. London Regt, as reinforcements.	
28/9/15.	Brigade Manoeuvres at Gt. Chishall and vicinity.	
29/9/15.	Camp Duties.	
30/9/15.	Battalion practised in Assault of Trenches.	
1/10/15.	Battalion practised in Digging in with Sandbags.	
2/10/15.	Kit & Foot Inspection, etc.	
3/10/15.	Divine Service.	
4/10/15.	Route March & Camp Duties.	

(Sd) R. DUNSMORE.　Lt. Colonel.
Comdg. 2/14th Bn. London Regt.
(London Scottish).

Army Form C. 2118.

WAR DIARY
or
INTELLIGENCE SUMMARY.
(Erase heading not required.)

October 1915. 2/14th. Battalion London Regiment. London Scottish.

Hour, Date, Place	Summary of Events and Information	Remarks and references to Appendices
October 1st.	Battalion practised in digging in, with sand-bags.	
" 2nd.	Kit, foot, and boot inspection in Camp.	
" 3rd.	Divine Service.	
" 4th.	Route march and Camp duties.	
" 5th.	Battalion left Camp for 4 days manoevres with 60th (London) Division. Arrived at Stebbing where Battalion proceeded to billets.	
" 6th.	Battalion in Brigade proceeded to Braintree and there took up a defensive position. Battalion billeted for the night at Braintree.	
" 7th.	Battalion in Brigade returned to Stebbing and there was billeted for the night.	
" 8th.	Battalion returned to Camp at Saffron Walden in conjuction with the 179th. Infantry Brigade.	
" 9th.	Kit and foot inspection in Camp.	

Instructions regarding War Diaries and Intelligence Summaries are contained in F.S.Regs., Part II. and the Staff Manual respectively. Title pages will be prepared in manuscript.

Army Form C. 2118.

WAR DIARY
or
INTELLIGENCE SUMMARY.

(Erase heading not required.)

2/14th. Battalion London Regiment.
London Scottish.

October 1915.

Hour, Date, Place	Summary of Events and Information	Remarks and references to Appendices
October 9th (Cont'd)	The following Officers detailed to attend the Divisional Range Finding Course at Bishops' Stortford. Instructor personnel. 2nd.Lieut.J.C.Miller. " " F.S.Thomson. " " J.S.Monro.	
" 10th.	Divine Service.	
" 11th.	Result of Divisional Machine Gun Course Bisley, published, N.C.Os and men:- 1st.Course First Class 3 Qualified.1. 2nd.Course " " 3 " 1.	
" 12th.	Battalion practiced attack on trenches. Result of Musketry Course Bisley Sept 13-Oct 1st., 1 N.C.O distinguished. Ex London Gazette :- Qmr Sgt P.H.Clephane to be Qmr with Hon. rank of Lieut. Aug.23 1915.	
" 13th.,	Information from Brigade Zeppelin passed over Saffron Walden in direction of London at 9 pm.	
" 14th.	Divisional exercise in the neighbourhood of Furneux Pelham. Battalion in attack on trenches after artillery preparat---."	

Army Form C. 2118.

WAR DIARY
or
INTELLIGENCE SUMMARY.
(Erase heading not required.)

October 1915.
2/14th Battalion London Regiment.
London Scottish.

Hour, Date, Place	Summary of Events and Information	Remarks and references to Appendices
October 14th (Cont'd)	Battalion billeted in Brent Pelham for the night.	
" 15th.	Battalion in Brigade returned to Saffron Walden.	
" 16th.	Kit and foot inspection. 2nd.Lieuts. Blackwell and W.Anderson. detailed for Divisional Range Finding Course, Bishops' Stortford. 18.10.15.	
" 17th.	Divine Service. Captain L.S.Lindsey Renton preceeded abroad to 1/14th Batt.B.E.F.	
" 18th.	Companies exercised in attack practice. 2nd.Lieut J.D.A.Mitchell detailed i/c Billeting party to Bishop' Stortford. Lieut.H.M.Clowes. detailed for Course of Instruction Camberley,25.10.15.	
" 19th.	Divisional Operations. Battalion marched in Brigade to Stebbing there billeted for the night.	
" 20th.	Divisional Operations cont'd.Battalion took up a defensive position at Cressing. Billeted at Braintree for the night.	

Army Form C. 2118.

WAR DIARY
or
INTELLIGENCE SUMMARY.
(Erase heading not required.)

October 1915.

2/14th.Battalion London Regiment.
London Scottish.

Instructions regarding War Diaries and Intelligence Summaries are contained in F.S.Regs., Part II. and the Staff Manual respectively. Title pages will be prepared in manuscript.

Hour, Date, Place	Summary of Events and Information	Remarks and references to Appendices
October 21st.	Divisional Operations cont'd. Battalion engaged in Rear-guard action. Billeted for the night at Stebbing.	
" 22nd.	Battalion in Brigade return to Saffron Walden.	
" 23rd.	Captain Cartwright to be Acting Major and Second in Command 23.10.15. Captain F.H.Lindsay transferred to 3rd.line Depot for Duty 18.10.15.	
" 24th.	Divine Service.	
" 25th.	Battalion engaged in clearing Camp previous to move to Bishops' Stortford on 26th.inst. Range Finding Course Bishops' Stortford, the following Officers qualified as Instructors:- 2nd.Lieut.J.S.Monro. " " F.S.Thompson. " " D.Blackwell. " " W.Anderson.	
" 26.	March to Bishops' Stortford with 179th.Infantry Brigade. Batt.Tommy.Headquarters Railway Hotel. Battalion billeted with Central Feeding.	

Army Form C. 2118.

WAR DIARY
or
INTELLIGENCE SUMMARY.

(Erase heading not required.)

2/14th Battalion London Regiment.
London Scottish.

October 1915.

Hour, Date, Place	Summary of Events and Information	Remarks and references to Appendices
October 26th. (Cont'd)	Ex London Gazette Lieut. A. Blaikie to be Tempy Captain with seniority next below Captain Ford.	
" 27th.	Battalion of General Fatigue duties. HQ. removed to "Rose Cottage". Station Road.	
" 28th.	Route March. Lieut. C.C. Taylor post i/c "B" Co. " "C" " Capt. A. Blaikie	
" 29th.	Concentration march. Captain L.D. Stubbs (M.O.) took over medical charge of 2/15th Batt., in addition to 2/14th. Conference at Bish ops' Stortford on recent manoevres.	
" 30th.	Kit and foot inspection.	
" 31st.	Divine Service.	

CONFIDENTIAL.

Army Form C. 2118.

WAR DIARY
or
INTELLIGENCE SUMMARY.
(Erase heading not required.)

Instructions regarding War Diaries and Intelligence Summaries are contained in F.S. Regs., Part II and the Staff Manual respectively. Title pages will be prepared in manuscript.

Hour, Date, Place	Summary of Events and Information	Remarks and references to Appendices
Nov.11th.15. Bps. Stortford.	Orders received from 60th.(London) Division that all Japanese rifles and ammunition be returned. .303 Long rifles issued.	R.
Nov.16th.15. Bps. Stortford.	Inspection of billets by G.O.C. 60th.(London) Division.	R.
Nov.22nd.15. Bps. Stortford.	Practice entraining and detraining started.	R.
Nov.25th.15. Bps. Stortford.	Inspection of Battalion by Colonel E.W.Baird Comdg.179th.Inf.Bde.	R.
Nov.30th.15. Bps. Stortford.	Detachment at Hertford relieved by the 2/15th.Battalion London Regt.	R.

Comdg. Lt.Colonel.

2/14th Bn. LONDON REGT.

C O N F I D E N T I A L.

War Diary of the

2/14th.Battalion, London Regiment, (London Scottish)

from 1st December 1915., to 30th., December 1915.

Army Form C. 2118.

WAR DIARY
or
INTELLIGENCE-SUMMARY.
(Erase heading not required.)

3/14th.Battalion London Regt,
London Scottish.

Instructions regarding War Diaries and Intelligence Summaries are contained in F.S. Regs., Part II. and the Staff Manual respectively. Title pages will be prepared in manuscript.

Hour, Date, Place	Summary of Events and Information	Remarks and references to Appendices
Bishops' Stortford.		
1st, December 1915.	Company and Platoon Drill under Lieut.C.C.Taylor. Signalling Section – Brigaded for Tactical Scheme.	R.W.
2nd. " "	Company training under Lt.H.M.Clowes. Officers in Signalling Instruction under Capt.Blaikie.	R.W.
3rd. " "	Prov.Company trained under 2nd.Lt.C.Wallis. Ex.London Gazette – Lieut.Clive Cornoch Taylor to be Tempy.Capt., with seniority as from 12 November 1914. 2nd.Lt.W.A.Tinlin,(Tempy Capt.) relinquishes the temporary rank of Capt. 2nd.Lieut.W.A.Tinlin to be temporary Lieut. dated 13.11.15.	R.W.
4th. " "	Prov.Company trained under 2nd.Lt.C.Wallis. Foot and Kit Inspection. N.C.O.and 3 men transferred to 104th. Prov.Battalion.	R.W.
5th. " "	Divine Service.	R.W.
6th. " "	A.,B., and C Companies under Capt.and Adjt.R.Whyte proceeded to Bombing ground, Hadham Hall for training. D. Company engaged in Guards and fatigues.	R.W.
7th. " "	Brigade concentration march to Much Hadham. Board convened today to perform stocktaking of various Ordnance Stores on charge of Companies, :- PRESIDENT. Capt.G.N.Ford. MEMBER. 2nd.Lt.Robertson. 2nd.Lt.D.N.Kennedy proceeded to Kelvedon for Course of Instruction in Trench Fighting.	R.W.

Army Form C. 2118.

WAR DIARY
or
INTELLIGENCE-SUMMARY.
(Erase heading not required.)

2/14th. Battalion London Regt.
London Scottish.

Hour, Date, Place	Summary of Events and Information	Remarks and references to Appendices
Bishops' Stortford.		
8th. December 1915.	Officer's Class in Visual Training under Lieut.H.Hunter. Companies exercised in Bombing practice under senior N.C.O's and Warrant officers. Practice emergency Alarm at 1pm carried through in accordance with Alarm Orders. 2nd.Lt.Liebert proceeded to Godstone for a Course of Instruction in Explosives.	R.W.
9th. "	Battalion exercised in Bombing under 2nd.Lt.Maclagan.	R.W.
10th. "	Night March. BN. comcentrated at Road Junction S of L in Blunts at 8pm., Ref.½" Ord.Map,Sheet 29. 2nd,Lt,T.D.O.Maclagan detailed as senior Bombing Officer in the BN.	R.W.
11th.December "	Battalion exercised in Bombing under 2nd.LT.Maclagan. Kit and Foot Inspection.	
12th. "	Divine Service.	
13th. "	BN.Exercised in Bombing under 2nd.Lt.Maclagan. 6 N.C.O's and 18 men in Miniature Range Course under Lt.Thomson. Eight Officers detailed for Riding School.	R.W.
14th. "	All available N.C.O's and men paraded for training under 2nd.Lt. Maclagan. Miniature Range Party under 2nd.Lieut.Hunter.	R.W.
15th. "	All available N.C.O' ad men paraded for training under 2nd.Lt.Maclagan. Specialists Sections under their own Officers.	R.W.

Army Form C. 2118.

WAR DIARY
or
INTELLIGENCE-SUMMARY.

2/14th.BN.London Regiment.
London Scottish.

(Erase heading not required.)

Instructions regarding War Diaries and Intelligence
Summaries are contained in F.S. Regs., Part II.
and the Staff Manual respectively. Title pages
will be prepared in manuscript.

Hour, Date, Place	Summary of Events and Information	Remarks and references to Appendices
Bishops' Stortford.		
16th. December 1915.	All available Officers attended a lecture on Trench Fighting by Captain H.C.Palmer. All available N.C.O's and men paraded from training under C.C.Taylor. 2nd.Lt.T.D.O.Maclagan, 3 N.C.O's and 17 men proceeded to Divisional Bombing School, Stansted for Instruction.	R.W.
17th. "	All available N.C.O's and men paraded for training under Lieut. W.A.Tinlin. Major H.S.Cartwright to be in temporary Command of the Battalion during the absence on leave of Lieut.Col.Dubsmore. Eight Officers transferred to 3/14th.Battalion. (Authority War Office letter 9/Infantry/2 T.FW3.).	R.W.
18th. "	All available N.C.O's and men paraded for training under Lieut.H.M. Clowes. Kit and foot inspection. Capt.D.D.Duncan took over command of 'A' Company as from 17th inst. Lieut.H.M.Clowes took over tempy command of 'B' Company as from 17th.	R.W.
19th. "	Divine Service.	
20th. "	Battalion Inspected by Major-General E.S.Bulfin, C.V.O., C.B., COMDG. 60th.(London) Division. Captain A.Blaikie detailed to attend Course of Instruction at Camberly Military College.	R.W.
21st. "	BN. paraded for training under 2nd.Lt.D.Blackwell. 6.N.C.O's and 18 men paraded for miniature range practice under 2nd. Lt.W.Anderson. Capt.D.D.Duncan,Lt.W.A.Tinlin.,Lt.H.M.Clowes, and Lt.H.Hunter visited School of Instruction in Military Engineering at Ongar.	R.W.

Army Form C. 2118.

WAR DIARY
or
INTELLIGENCE SUMMARY — 2/14th.BN.London Regiment.
London Scottish.

(*Erase heading not required.*)

Instructions regarding War Diaries and Intelligence Summaries are contained in F.S. Regs., Part II. and the Staff Manual respectively. Title pages will be prepared in manuscript.

Hour, Date, Place	Summary of Events and Information	Remarks and references to Appendices
Bishops' Stortford.		
22nd. December 1916.	BN. Paraded for training under the Adjutant. Lieut. H. Hunter proceeded to Kelvedon for a Course in Trench Fighting.	H.W.
23rd. "	All available N.C.O's and men paraded for training under Capt. D.D. Duncan. Scouts and Machine Gunners under their own Officers.	R.W.
24th. "	Lt. Col. R. Dunsmore returned from leave and resumes Command of the BN. Company Training - Scouts, Signallers and M.G. under their own Officers.	R.W.
25th. "	Church Parade and Divine Service.	R.W.
26th. "	Divine Service.	
27th. "	3 N.C.O's and 14 men under 2nd.LT.S.G.Wilson, proceeded to Div. Bomb. School, Stansted for Instruction. -- Holiday.	R.W.
28th. "	BN. Concentration march. Point of Concentration - Road junction W of S in NETHER STREET, near WIDFORD. Ref. ½" Ord. Map. Sheet 29.	R.W.
29th. "	Battalion exercised in Close order drill - Officers tactical exercise without Troops.	R.W.
30th. "	Battalion exercised in attack on and clearing of a village.	R.W.
31st. "	Training under Platoon Commanders.	

COPY.   APPENDIX 'A'.

179th Infantry Brigade.

CONCENTRATION MARCH.

Tuesday 7th December 1915.

Reference:- Ord.Survey Raining Sheet No.29. BISHOPS' STORTFORD.
             1.inch. - 2 miles.   4th.December 1915.

The 179th Infantry Brigade will concentrate on LITTLE HADHAM - WIDFORD Road facing SOUTH - head of column at road junction WEST of C in HADHAM CROSS, at 12 o'clock noon on Tuesday 7th December 1915 in the following order :-

    2/15th. Battalion.
    2/13th. Battalion.
    2/14th. Battalion.

Companies will concentrate to Battalions at the following points.

2/13th Battalion concentration point - Road bend WEST of first T in THORLEY STREET.

2/14th. Battalion concentration point - Cross roads SOUTH of O in SRANDON.

2/15th Battalion concentration point - Road junction EAST of point 182 on BARWICK - HADHAM CROSS Road.

Transport fully loaded will accompany battalions, sufficient being left behind to deal with supplies.

A haversack ration will ~~supplies~~ carried.

                  BY ORDER.

                  B.LEVETT.

        CAPTAIN & BRIGADE MAJOR.

        179th Infantry Brigade.

2/4 London Regt

WAR DIARY
or
INTELLIGENCE SUMMARY.
(Erase heading not required.)

Army Form C. 2118.

Instructions regarding War Diaries and Intelligence Summaries are contained in F.S. Regs., Part II. and the Staff Manual respectively. Title pages will be prepared in manuscript.

Hour, Date, Place		Summary of Events and Information	Remarks and references to Appendices
1.1.16.	Bishops Stortford.	All available N.C.O's and men paraded for training under Lieut. N.H. Cowles. Kit and foot inspection. Lieut J.C. Miller appointed officer in charge of 149th Infantry Brigade Range for this Course. Lieut N. Hunter and 2nd Lieut S.G. Wilson detailed for this Course.	
10.a.m. 2.1.16.	"	Church Parade	
3.1.16.	"	Company Close Order drill under Company Commanders, including Marching on points. 2nd Lieut Blackroll left for a Course of Musketry at Bisley.	
4.1.16.	"	Battalion Route March with Scheme. Advance Guard. No operation orders were issued.	
5.1.16.	"	Battalion Drill under Adjutant. All officers. Close Defence of a farm. 2nd Lieut Anderson left for a Course of Field Engineering at Cryor.	
6.1.16	"	Battalion. Close defence of a farm. Piggotts farm one mile S.W. of Bishops Stortford on the Much Hadham road. Retired in Northerly direction on Stortford on the Little Hadham road. No operation orders were issued. The Bombing Officer 2nd Lieut Mackayan tried his trench Mortars made from a drain pipe. With Salvo factory results.	

Army Form C. 2118.

WAR DIARY
or
INTELLIGENCE SUMMARY.
(Erase heading not required.)

Instructions regarding War Diaries and Intelligence Summaries are contained in F.S. Regs., Part II. and the Staff Manual respectively. Title pages will be prepared in manuscript.

Hour, Date, Place	Summary of Events and Information	Remarks and references to Appendices
7.1.16. Bishops Stortford.	Battalion Convoy Scheme, Bishops Stortford, Spellbrook, Exnell's Farm 8½ miles.	
8.1.16 "	Battalion paraded under Lieut H.M. Clowes for training. Kit and foot inspection. A draft of 32 men from the Administrative Centre join the Battalion this day.	
10 A.M. 9.1.16 "	Church Parade.	
10.1.16 "	All available men paraded under 2nd Lieut Maclagan for Bombing. 2nd Lieut S.G. Kitson detailed for Riding School.	
11.1.16 "	The Battalion paraded under 2nd Lieut Maclagan for the purpose of filling in trenches.	
12.1.16 "	309 men from the 3/14th B. East Kent, joined the Battalion this day. 2nd Lieut J.A. Thomas approved Machine Gun Officer to date 1st Jan.y 1916.	
13.1.16 "	The Battalion paraded under 2nd Lieut J.D.O. Maclagan for filling in trenches at Moa Lodge. 15 men joined the Battalion this day from the Administrative Centre.	
14.1.16 "	Battalion under 2nd Lieut J.D.O. Maclagan for filling in trenches at Moa Lodge.	

Army Form C. 2118.

WAR DIARY
or
INTELLIGENCE SUMMARY.
(Erase heading not required.)

Instructions regarding War Diaries and Intelligence Summaries are contained in F.S. Regs., Part II. and the Staff Manual respectively. Title pages will be prepared in manuscript.

Hour, Date, Place	Summary of Events and Information	Remarks and references to Appendices
14.1.16. Bishops Stortford.	Capt. J.R. Duncan, Lieut Mitchell, and 2nd Lieuts Wilson, Hill and Paterson joined this Battalion this day. Extract from the London Gazette dated 14.1.16. 2nd Lieut W. Anderson and 2nd Lieut C.F. Burn of this Battalion were awarded the D.C.M.	
15.1.16 "	Company training, Kit and Foot inspection.	
16.1.16 "	Church Parade. Presbyterians 9.45. a.m. Church of England 9. a.m.	
17.1.16 "	All available N.C.O.'s and men paraded under 2nd Lieut T.D.O. Maclagan for filling in trenches at Alsa Lodge.	
18.1.16 "	All available N.C.O.'s and men paraded under 2nd Lt. Wallis, for filling in trenches at Alsa Lodge. Medical inspection of Recruits completed. 2nd Lt. S.G. Wilson appointed Assistant Transport Officer.	
19.1.16 "	All available N.C.O.'s and men paraded under 2nd Lieut Wallis for filling in trenches at Alsa Lodge. Bombers paraded under 2nd Lt. Maclagan. 2nd Lieut M.B. Liebert returned from Godstone.	

(73989) W4141—463. 400,000. 9/14. H.&J.Ltd. Forms/C. 2118/10.

WAR DIARY
or
INTELLIGENCE SUMMARY.
(Erase heading not required.)

Army Form C. 2118.

Instructions regarding War Diaries and Intelligence Summaries are contained in F.S. Regs., Part II. and the Staff Manual respectively. Title pages will be prepared in manuscript.

Hour, Date, Place	Summary of Events and Information	Remarks and references to Appendices
20.1.16 Bishops Stortford	Battalion paraded under Captⁿ H. A. Iselin for Training & Route March. Advance party under Lieut N. M. Clarkes proceeded to Sutton Veny near Warminster.	
21.1.16 "	Battalion on fatigue duties cleaning Billets. Rear party under 2nd Lieut W.B. Lillett paraded at 9 a.m. N.B. Companies paraded at 12 midnight (21/22) under the C.O. for entraining for Sutton Veny. Dress:- Marching Order, overcoats worn. 100 Rounds of Ammunition carried. Each man carried his Kit bag. 2nd Lieut R. M. Robertson to act as Rost R.T.O. for 1st Train. 2nd Lieut T. D. O. Maclagan " " " 2nd Train. 2nd Lieut J. S. Norris " Adjutant of 2nd Train.	
22.1.16 "	A & B. Companies entrained at 12.45 A.M. for No 9 Camp, Sutton Veny under the C.O. C & D. Companies entrained at 2.45 A.M. under Major Cartwright.	
22.1.16 Sutton Veny	A & B. Companies arrived Warminster at 9 A.M. Kit bags were filed in Station yard. Lieut N. M. Clarke in charge of the advance party met train and acted as guide to N° 9 Camp, Sutton Veny. C & D. Companies arrived 9.10 A.M., 2nd Lieut Barker acted as guide for this party.	

Army Form C. 2118.

WAR DIARY
or
INTELLIGENCE SUMMARY.
(Erase heading not required.)

Instructions regarding War Diaries and Intelligence Summaries are contained in F.S. Regs., Part II. and the Staff Manual respectively. Title pages will be prepared in manuscript.

Hour, Date, Place	Summary of Events and Information	Remarks and references to Appendices
23.1.16. Sutton Veny.	Church Parade for all denominations 10. A.M. 2nd Lieut Colin Burn joined the Battalion this day.	
24.1.16 " "	The Battalion paraded under Major Cartwright for training. Specialists paraded for training under their own Officers. Lecture by Col. Nash on Interior Economy to all officers at 4.30.	
25.1.16 " "	Battalion paraded under the C.O. for a route march. Captain N. Buchanan detailed to attend Grenade Course at Clapham on 31st inst.	
26.1.16 " "	The Battalion paraded at 8.30 for Inspection by General the Rt. Hon. Sir Arthur Paget, G.C.B., M.C.V.O.	
27.1.16 " "	All available Officers to assemble in Officers Mess at 9. a.m. for field Sketching under 2nd Lt. O. Still. Recruits paraded at 9 a.m. under the Assistant Acting Adjutant. Battalion paraded in huts at 9 a.m. for training under their own Officers. Specialists under their own Officers. Lecture to all Officers by the Machine Gun Officer.	
28.1.16 " "	The Battalion paraded for a Route March to Hammersmith.	

(73989) W4141—463. 400,000. 9/14. H.&J.Ltd. Forms/C. 2118/10.

Army Form C. 2118.

WAR DIARY
or
INTELLIGENCE SUMMARY.
(Erase heading not required.)

Instructions regarding War Diaries and Intelligence Summaries are contained in F. S. Regs., Part II. and the Staff Manual respectively. Title pages will be prepared in manuscript.

Hour, Date, Place	Summary of Events and Information	Remarks and references to Appendices
28.1.16. Authie Very	Extract from London Gazette 28.1.1916	
	Capt A. Blaikie to be temporary Major dated 28.1.1916	
	Lieut W. A. Julin " " " Captain " " "	
	Lieut J. M. Clarke " " " Captain " " "	
	Lieut N. Hunter " " " Captain " " "	
	2nd Lieut W. A. Lillet " " " Lieut " " 6.11.1915	
	2nd Lieut W. A. Lillet takes precedence next above Lt. B. Fotting without pay and allowances prior to 28.1.1916.	
	2nd Lieut J. S. Munro to be temporary Lieut dated 28.1.1916	
	2nd Lieut J. W. Brooke " " " " " "	
	2nd Lieut L. C. B. Booker " " " " " "	
	Lecture to all Officers on Machine Gun by Machine Gun Officer.	
29.1.16 " "	Kit and foot inspection. All kits were washed out.	
	A Court of Inquiry was held in the lecture room at 10.15 to enquire into the circumstances attending the injury to Rifle No. 1469.	
	President Capt J. L. Duncan	
	Members { Lieut J. W. Brooke	
	{ 2nd Lieut C. Wallis	

Army Form C. 2118.

WAR DIARY
or
INTELLIGENCE SUMMARY.
(Erase heading not required.)

Instructions regarding War Diaries and Intelligence Summaries are contained in F.S. Regs., Part II. and the Staff Manual respectively. Title pages will be prepared in manuscript.

Hour, Date, Place	Summary of Events and Information	Remarks and references to Appendices
30.1.16. Sutton Veny	Church Parade. Presbyterians 6:40. Church of England 10:25. The C.O. inspected all huts.	
31.1.16 "	The Battalion, as strong as possible, paraded for inspection of the 60th (London) Division by Field Marshall Viscount French G.C.B. O.M. G.C.V.O., K.C.M.G., at 1.30. Lecture to all officers by the M.O. on Camp Sanitation at 5.30	

Lieutenant Colonel
Commanding 2/the 15th Battalion London Regiment

C O N F I D E N T I A L.

War Diary of the :-

2/14th. Battalion London Regiment (London Scottish.)

From Feb.1st 1916 to Feb 29th. 1916.

Army Form C. 2118.

WAR DIARY
or
INTELLIGENCE SUMMARY.
(Erase heading not required.)

Instructions regarding War Diaries and Intelligence Summaries are contained in F.S. Regs., Part II. and the Staff Manual respectively. Title pages will be prepared in manuscript.

Hour, Date, Place	Summary of Events and Information	Remarks and references to Appendices
1st.Feb.1916 Sutton Veny.	Parade at 7-30 a.m. under Platoon Commanders for running exercise squad drill. Parade at 9 am under O.C.Coys for training. Battalion parade for route march at 11 am. Route - LONGBRIDGE DEVERILL - the turning below the B in PARSONAGE BARN - SHEARCROSS. 25 short H.L.L.E. rifles were issued to each Coy.	SWB
2/2/16 do	Parade at 7-30 am under Platoon Commanders. Battalion parade at 9 am for training. 11-12 noon - Musketry Instruction. 2 pm Battalion parade - Platoon Commanders Lieut. J.S.Monro & 2nd.Lt. A.C.Wilson detailed to attend a Lewis Gun Course at Hayling Island on the 14th inst. The G.O.C. expressed his pleasure to all ranks for the way they carried themselves at the inspection on the 31st.ulto.	
3/2/16. do	Parade at 7-30 am under platoon Commanders. Coys paraded at 9 am for training under Coy Commanders.. Musketry Instruction 11-12 noon. Parade 2 pm for training under Platoon Commanders. Lecture to all Officers at 5-40 pm on the duties of an Officer by Col. Nash. Week end leave granted to 5% of the Battalion.	
4/2/16. do	Parade as on the 3rd. inst. The rear party 20 strong in Command of Lieut. Liebert returned this day. Lecture to all N.C.Os by the M.O. on Camp Sanitation.	
5/2/16. do	Parade under platoon Commanders at 7-30 am. Companies under O.C.Coys. for training and close order drill. All huts washed out. Kit and foot inspection. A draft of 62 men from the 3/14th.Bn. at East Sheen joined this day. Lieut. J.C.Miller appointed Assistant Adjt. vice Capt. H.Hunter to duty.	
6/2/16. do	Church parade. Presbyterians 8-45 am. Church of England 10-30 am. Parade under platoon Commanders at 7-30 am for running exercise and squad drill. Parade under O.C.Coys at 9 am, for training. Musketry instruction 11-12 noon. Platoons under platoon commanders at 2 pm. 3 pm lecture on care of arms - saluting. 2nd.Lt. D.Blackwell and Serg. F.D.Chappell obtained distinguished at school of musketry, Bisley at the course which started on 3rd.Jan.16. Sgt. R.L.Ogg obtained distinguished at the 3rd. Army School for	
7/2/16.		

Army Form C. 2118.

WAR DIARY
or
INTELLIGENCE SUMMARY.
(Erase heading not required.)

Instructions regarding War Diaries and Intelligence Summaries are contained in F.S. Regs., Part II. and the Staff Manual respectively. Title pages will be prepared in manuscript.

Hour, Date, Place	Summary of Events and Information	Remarks and references to Appendices
8/2/16. Sutton Veny.	Signalling. Lectures to all Officers on care of arms by the Assistant Adjt. at 6 pm.	
	Parade under platoon commanders at 7-30 am. Battalion paraded under the C.O. for route march. Route - LONGBRIDGE DEVERILL, turning below B in PARSONAGE BARN - SHEARCROSS. Parade under platoon commanders at 2 pm. Lecture to all Officers on Indication and recognition by the Assistant adjt. at 6 pm. A small fire occurred in Hut No.17. Slight damage was done.	
9/2/16. do	Parade under platoon Commanders, at 7-30 am. Parade under O.C.Coys at 9 am for training. Lecture on indication and recognition 11-12 noon. Parade under platoon commanders at 2 pm. Court of enquiry assembled to enquire into the loss of certain equipment. President Major H.S.Cartwright, Members:- Lieuts. Liebert & Bowker. The following Officers passed out of the riding school :- Capts. H.Buchanan & H.M.Clowes.	

Army Form C. 2118.

WAR DIARY
or
INTELLIGENCE SUMMARY.
(Erase heading not required.)

Instructions regarding War Diaries and Intelligence Summaries are contained in F.S. Regs., Part II. and the Staff Manual respectively. Title pages will be prepared in manuscript.

Hour, Date, Place	Summary of Events and Information	Remarks and references to Appendices
10.2.16 Sutton Veny	Parade under Platoon Commanders 7.30 a.m. for squad drill and running exercise. Parade under O.C. Companies 9 a.m. for training. Lecture 11 - 12. Noon Elementary Musketry to Recruits. Parade under Platoon Commanders at 2 p.m. Lecture to all N.C.O's by 2nd Lt. R.M. Robertson on Platoon Drill. Pte Goddard removed to Hospital today.	
11.2.16 Sutton Veny	Parade under Platoon Commanders 7.30 a.m. for squad drill and running exercise. Parade under Os C. Companies 9.0 a.m. for training. Lecture 11 - 12. Elementary Musketry to Recruits. Parade under platoon commanders at 2. p.m.. Owing to the rain in the morning, training was carried on in the Huts.	
12.2.16 SuttonVeny.	Parade under Platoon Commanders 7.30 a.m. squad drill and running exercise. 9 a.m. to 12 noon Companies were at the disposal of the O.C. Companies. Kit and Foot inspection were carried and also ½ hour each Physical Training and close order drill were carriedout. The huts were scrubbed out during the morning. In the afternoon the Battalion team was successful in a Rugby Football match against Capt. Moncrieff's 15, by 20 points to 12, and also in an association match against the Queen's Westminsters, by 8 goals to 1. Pte S.Goddard 6314 reported to have died at Isolation Hospital Salisbury (by telegram) 3 officers left for course at Hayling Island to report before 5 p.m.	
13.2.16. Sutton Veny	DIVINE SERVICES Lt.Col. R.Dunsmore left for France to join B.E.F. for instruction at 11. a.m. this morning	

Army Form C. 2118.

WAR DIARY
or
INTELLIGENCE SUMMARY.
(Erase heading not required.)

Instructions regarding War Diaries and Intelligence Summaries are contained in F.S. Regs., Part II. and the Staff Manual respectively. Title pages will be prepared in manuscript.

Hour, Date, Place	Summary of Events and Information	Remarks and references to Appendices
14. February 1916	Parade 7.30a.m. under Platoon Commanders and remainder of days parades as per Friday except that a Miniature range party paraded under Sgt. Fullerton E.A. and a musketry party under the Assistant Adjutant. Reveille was at 6 today and not 6.30a.m. 7th Xmas leave party left Camp at 7.10a.m. today. Sgt. Major Grant left Battallion this day. Lecture to all Officers in the Mess at 6p.m. on "Inter communication" by the Signalling Officer, Assistant Adjutant lectures to all N.C.O's of Musketry at 5.30.p.m. Major H.S.Cartwright assumed command of Battallion in C.O's absence 13/2/16.	
15 February 1916	Parade 7.30a.m. under Platoon Commanders. 9a.m. parade of all available N.C.O's and men under Capt. D.D.Duncan, for practice in attack. Recruits paraded for training as per programme issued. All Signallers paraded for training at 9.a.m. (including Company Signallers) Court of Inquiry was held regarding fire in No17 Hut No. 9 Camp. An Aircraft alarm was given in the Camp at 7.p.m. this evening when 2½mins. were taken to extinguish all lights in Camp.	
16 " "	Battallion was paraded to move off to Divisional Scheme; but parade was cancelled on account of bad weather. Training was carried out according to programme as from 9.a.m. Bad weather more or less prevented outdoor training so lectures in and training in the Huts was carried out.	

WAR DIARY or INTELLIGENCE SUMMARY.

(Erase heading not required.)

Army Form C. 2118.

Instructions regarding War Diaries and Intelligence Summaries are contained in F.S. Regs., Part II and the Staff Manual respectively. Title pages will be prepared in manuscript.

Hour, Date, Place	Summary of Events and Information	Remarks and references to Appendices
17.2.16. Sutton Veny.	Reveille 5 am. Breakfast 6 am. Parade:- Head of Battalion passed Battalion Headquarters at 7 am en route for Starling Point for Div. Scheme. 16 men transferred to the 104th.Provisional Battalion.TF.	
18.2.16. do	Parade 7-30 am. under platoon commanders as usual. Rain prevented early outdoor training. Night work ordered for to-day, was cancelled. 1st.line transport was inspected by Major General Landon CB. at Greenhill House to-day at 10 am. O.C.Coys paid their Coys. Trained men of C Coy fired the preliminary 10 rounds course today. 3 Officers and 3 men transferred to Div. Cyclist Coy dated 9/2/16.	
19.2.16. do	Parade as usual under platoon commanders at 7-30 am. 9 am to 12 noon kit and foot inspection was carried out. Floors of all huts were scrubbed and windows cleaned. Week end leave party left camp at 12-5 pm.	
20.2.16. do	Divine Service. Hut inspection by C.O. at 11-30 am. Lt. Colonel R.Dunsmore returned to-day and resumed command of the Battalion.	
21.2.16. do	Parade as usual at 7-30 am under platoon commanders. All available N.C.Os and Men (trained.) paraded at 9 am under Major A.Blaikie. All huts were inspected Horses inspected by the Inspector of Remounts in the Camp at 12-20 pm. 6 pm. C.O. lectured to all Officers on his experiences at the front with the BEF.	
22.2.16. do	Parade as usual under platoon commanders at 7-30 am. 9 am. Trained men parade under Major a Blaikie for training. Fire direction was carried out in Miniature range, to-day at 3-30 pm. by N.C.Os. MO. lectured to Sanitary Sect., Stretcher Bearers, Drummers and Buglers in his hut to-day. Parties of trained men fired preliminary Course on open range Lieut. M.Murphy 2nd. Bn.Royal Welch Fusiliers is attached to this Bn.	
23.2.16. do	Parade at 7-30 am as usual, for doublingunder platoon commanders. 9 am trained men paraded under Major aBlaikie for outpost scheme.Fire direction practice carried out at 3-30 pm. in Miniature range. Lecture to all Officers on experiencies at the front with BEF. at 6 pm. Lecture to all N.C.Os on Musketry by the Assistant Adjt.	
24.2.16. do	Parade at 7-30 am as usual under Platoon Commanders. Trained men & recruits parade to-day as yesterday.	

Army Form C. 2118.

WAR DIARY
or
INTELLIGENCE SUMMARY.
(Erase heading not required.)

Instructions regarding War Diaries and Intelligence Summaries are contained in F.S. Regs., Part II. and the Staff Manual respectively. Title pages will be prepared in manuscript.

Hour, Date, Place	Summary of Events and Information	Remarks and references to Appendices
25.2.16. Sutton Veny.	Miniature range was used throughout the day and fire direction was practised by 5 N.C.Os under Musketry Officer. No training in the afternoon. Parade 6 pm for night outposts for trained men and night march for recruits. 4 men transferred to the 3/14th.Bn.Lon.Regt. (London Scottish.) & 2 to 104th.Provisional Battalion TF. Parade at 7-30 am as usual under Platoon Commanders. 9-10 am Physical Training & Bayonet fighting. Parade at 10-30 am for rute march with advanced guard,Rear guard, & Flank guard Route taken - No.9 Camp on Sutton V ny Longbridge Deverill Road to corner N of Lower Barn Farm - Shear Water - Shear Cross- Longbridge Deverill No.9 Camp. Platoons were at disposal of Platoon Commanders from 2-3 pm to-day. Coys were paid to-day.	
26.2.16. do	Heavy snow fall on night 25/26th.Feb.16 necessitated the postponing of the Saturday training owing to a large extent. Large parties were required to clean the roads and lines in the Camp. Huts were scrubbed out and foot inspection was carried out. Miniature range was carried out from 9 am by 20 men.	
27.2.16. do	Divine Service. Hut inspection by C.O. at 11 am.	
28.2.16. do	Parade at 7-30 am as usual under platoon commanders for running exercise. Recruits musketry class paraded under 2nd.Lt. D.Blackwell N.C.Os Musketry Class under 2nd.Lt. C.Wallis, assembled at 10 am. Miniature range practice was carried out from 9 am. Recruits and trained men paraded at 9 am and 2 pm for training. M.O. lectures to Sanitary Section,Stretcher Bearers,Buglers and drummers in his hut at 3 pm to-day. Lecture by M.G.O. at 6 pm. in mess on Lewis Gun. 9th. Xmas leave party left camp at 6-45 am this morning.	

Army Form C. 2118.

WAR DIARY
or
INTELLIGENCE SUMMARY.
(Erase heading not required.)

Instructions regarding War Diaries and Intelligence Summaries are contained in F.S. Regs., Part II. and the Staff Manual respectively. Title pages will be prepared in manuscript.

Hour, Date, Place	Summary of Events and Information	Remarks and references to Appendices
29.2.16. Sutton Veny.	Parade at 7-30 am as usual under platoon Commanders. At 9 am and 2 pm. Trained men and recruits paraded separately. 100 men (recruits) and employed men fired the 10 rounds preliminary musketry course today. N.C.Os Musketry Insyruction Class as usual .M.O. lectures to Sanitary Sect., Stretcher Bearers, Buglers & Drummers at 3 pm. Miniature range practice was carried out throughout the day from 9 am.	

Confidential.

War Diary of
2/14th Battalion London Regiment.
(London Scottish)

from 1st March 1916 to 31st March 1916.

Volume

Army Form C. 2118.

WAR DIARY
or
INTELLIGENCE SUMMARY.
(Erase heading not required.)

Instructions regarding War Diaries and Intelligence Summaries are contained in F.S. Regs., Part II. and the Staff Manual respectively. Title pages will be prepared in manuscript.

Hour, Date, Place	Summary of Events and Information	Remarks and references to Appendices
1.3.16 Sutton Veny	Parade 7.30am under Platoon Commanders for doubling whilst exercise. Trained men and recruits paraded at 8.45am under Capt. D.A. Duncan. Route march was taken. Rifle ragging was carried out. At 9am to 12pm Trained men recruits together for recruit training. Miniature range practice was carried out through the day from 9am. Lt. N. Huxley & Rev. Sulet Hamlin attached this Battalion reported to all WOs & NCOs at 5.15pm on the MONS operation. 2 men transferred to 3/1st Battn. London Regt -1- & 10th Pier Battn.	SAP SAP SAP SAP SAP
2.3.16 "	Parade 7.30am on usual under Platoon Commanders 9.15-10am Regimental Training. Bayonet fighting was carried out. 10.30am Battn Paraded for Route march with advanced guard etc. Route taken:- No 9 CAMP along SUTTON VENY – LONGBRIDGE DEVERIL road to corner N. of LONER. BARN Fm — halted 35min. 500 yds S. of hour 1.99. SHEARWATER – SHEAR CROSS. – LONGBRIDGE DEVERIL – No 9 CAMP. Miniature Rifle range was used throughout the day from 9am. R. Sergt Major received at all NCOs class of A/Sergt today at 5.15pm No 3485 A.Sgt R.S.M. William E. Sawin (late of this Battalion) has been awarded the "Medaille Militaire" for distinguished service during the campaign. (Extract London Gazette 23.2.16)	SAP SAP SAP SAP
3.3.16 "	Parade 7.30am as usual under Platoon Commanders for musketry exercise. 9am to 12pm Recruits trained men paraded together for Recruit Training. At 1.15pm a party paraded under Capt. McBuchanan for digging machine Gunner paraded separately under senior NCO for training. Miniature Range was used throughout the day from 9am. Captain Bollin Leaving 6. Cy Commander and leaves on Command on Protection on the hours at 4.5am. MO relieves to Sanitary Sector. 9am today. 10 men transferred to 10th Pier. Battn 15 day.	SAP SAP

WAR DIARY or INTELLIGENCE SUMMARY.

(Erase heading not required.)

Army Form C. 2118.

Instructions regarding War Diaries and Intelligence Summaries are contained in F. S. Regs., Part II. and the Staff Manual respectively. Title pages will be prepared in manuscript.

Hour, Date, Place	Summary of Events and Information	Remarks and references to Appendices
1.3.16 Sutton Veny	Parade 9.30am under Platoon Commanders for marching order inspection. Capt J. D. Pearson inspected at 9.45am. The whole men were thoroughly and carried out. At 9pm Coy heard lecture from men coming together for the first time from various training Camps to all men coming together to meet the Battalion lectures to all ranks. 2pm Platoon R.A.M.C. parade Lectures NOTCs etc 5.15pm on M. NCOs duties. 2 men transferred to 3rd Batt. Inoculated -2 to 10st Pro 13 men.	SNP SNP SNP SNP SNP
2.3.16 "	Parade 9.30am as usual under Platoon Commanders 9.15-10am Physical exercise. 10.30am Bath Parade Bayonet fighting run completed out. Route march :– No 9 Camp Dressing with advanced guard etc. No 9 LOWER for Route march :– SUTTON VENY – LONGBRIDGE DEVERIL next to arrive No 9 LOWER LONG SUTTON VENY – LONGBRIDGE DEVERIL 5.pm Sqt Major L.H. SPEAR WATER – SHEAR BARN FM – halted 35 mins. 500 yds Sqt Major L.H. SPEAR WATER – SHEAR CROSS – LONGBRIDGE DEVERIL – No 9 CAMP. Inoculation to an day from 9am to 5.15pm Musketry Rifle exam were read of 4 Kings today at 5.15pm R. Saythorpe W. Listed to all NCOs on Rank of (the Battalion) has been specified SNP No 3105 Adj R.S.M Norman C. Sewart etc, if the Battalion has been specified SNP the "N.C.O.R. Initiative" is distinguished wishes during the campaign (Student SNP (-.am-Iga 22.3.16)	SNP
3.3.16 "	Parade 9.30am as usual under Platoon Commanders for marching order Lectures 9pm & 2pm Recruits started training under Capt N.Benbow to officer for Recruit Training. At 1.15pm a Paty [indicates under Capt N.Benbow to officer for digging machine Gunners] [indecipherable] by [indecipherable] under Sergt NCO to training Practice Range was used. We ought to stay for grain. Captain Bolton lectured to Coy Commanders and Bombers on Bayonet Platoon, in to train at 4pm. NC. Lecture to Sanitary Section at 3pm today SWS. 10 new Recruits to Coy from Pte Jetfin today	S.S.

Army Form C. 2118.

WAR DIARY
or
INTELLIGENCE SUMMARY.
(Erase heading not required.)

Instructions regarding War Diaries and Intelligence Summaries are contained in F. S. Regs., Part II. and the Staff Manual respectively. Title pages will be prepared in manuscript.

Hour, Date, Place	Summary of Events and Information	Remarks and references to Appendices
4.3.16 Sutton Veny	Parade 7.30am for donning overcoat under Platoon Commanders. From 9am all men Kit inspection was carried out as also the marking of huts & hour each close order drill. Physical training. Lt. Nelson-Young & L./Sgts. Manners qualified at the Lewis Gun Course Hayling Island (1.3.16)	SAP. SAP. SAP.
5.3.16 "	Parade - Divine Service. Hut inspection by C.O. at 11.30am	SAP.
6.3.16 "	Parade 7.30am as usual under Platoon Commanders. 9am till 12 noon Battalion drill under C.O. 1.25pm digging party paraded. 50 men paraded for Bombing instruction under 2/Lt. T.R.O. Maclagan a miniature. 7.30pm Night work was carried out. 52 men paraded for Bombing instruction under Bombing instructors.	SAP. SAP.
7.3.16 "	Parade 7.30am as usual under Platoon Commanders. Parade 9am & 2pm. Recruits strained new paraded for training in marching order. Miniature Range was used by 20 N.C.O's men during whole day Stretcher Bearer paraded for training as a section. M.O. lecture to all officers on First-Aid at 6pm also at 3pm to the Sanitary Section. Bombers paraded today as yesterday (SAP)	SAP. SAP. SAP. SAP. SAP. & SAP.
8.3.16 " "	Retreat was played by Brigade wide Bands in the Camp today	SAP

Army Form C. 2118.

WAR DIARY
or
INTELLIGENCE SUMMARY.
(Erase heading not required.)

Instructions regarding War Diaries and Intelligence Summaries are contained in F.S. Regs., Part II and the Staff Manual respectively. Title pages will be prepared in manuscript.

Hour, Date, Place	Summary of Events and Information	Remarks and references to Appendices
4.3.16 Sutton Veny	Parade 9.30am for drilling carried out under Platoon Commanders. 9am till noon Intersection was carried out as also its marking of huts & barracks also order close order Physical Training. Finkley-Young & R75 marched to billeted at the Cairo Gen Annex Heytesbury Islands (1.3.16)	SNP SNP SNP
5.3.16 "	Parade & Divine Service. Hut inspection by C.O. at 11.30am	SNP SNP
6.3.16 "	Parade 9.30am & recruit were Platoon Commanders, 9am till 12 noon Battalion drill under C.O. 1.25pm digging fatigue paraded. 50 men paraded for bombing instruction under 2/Lt T.R.C. Molyneaux & anoth also. 4.25pm Sergt-Instr were assembled and 52 non commissions paraded for Bombing instruction under Batt Bombing officer & non Platoon Commanders	SNP SNP SNP SNP SNP SNP
7.3.16 "	Parade 7.30am on musketry drill 9am & 2pm Recruits attended new parades for training in Marching order. Ammunition Returns were made by 20 NCOs. Drawn during whole day. Brown Blown paraded for training on a section. NO Officers or other ranks any First Aid at 1pm also at 3pm to do Sanitary Section. Rubel was played by Brigade massed Bands in this Camp today. Bombers paraded today as yesterday.	SNP SNP SNP SNP SNP SNP

Army Form C. 2118.

WAR DIARY
or
INTELLIGENCE SUMMARY.
(Erase heading not required.)

Instructions regarding War Diaries and Intelligence Summaries are contained in F. S. Regs., Part II. and the Staff Manual respectively. Title pages will be prepared in manuscript.

Hour, Date, Place	Summary of Events and Information	Remarks and references to Appendices
8.3.16. Sutton Veny.	Parade under Platoon Commanders at 7.15 a.m. for doubling exercise. This parade was cancelled owing to parties being required for clearing snow from roads. 9–10 a.m. Physical Training. Bayonet Fighting. Battalion paraded for Route march with protection. Route taken:— No 9 CAMP on SUTTON VENY, LONGBRIDGE DEVERIL Rd — N to CROCKERTON — W to corner S of S in BUCKLERS WOOD — NE to crossroad at BORE HILL — S to point 400 — E through SOUTHLEIGH WOOD to No 9 CAMP. Rifle & Foot inspection was carried out on return to camp. Miniature range was used by 20 men throughout the day. Bombing class as usual.	S.A.P. S.A.P. S.A.P. S.A.P. S.A.P.
9.3.16. Sutton Veny.	Parade 7.15 a.m. as usual under Platoon Commanders for doubling & drill exercises. 9 a.m. – 2 p.m. trained new recruits together for training. 180 men paraded for digging at 8.55 a.m. under Capt H.W.B. Lewis. Party fired 1st practice (50 yds & 100 yds) on open range during the morning. Miniature range was used throughout the day by 20 men & 6 NCOs. Bombers paraded as usual. Night punt was carried out. Platoon Concentration march on points of Cross Tracks intersected by 400 ft contour line due S of Mt L and LITTLECOMBE HILL (Ref 1" Ord Sheet 122) Time of Concentration 9 a.m.	S.A.P. S.A.P. S.A.P.

WAR DIARY or INTELLIGENCE SUMMARY

Army Form C. 2118.

Hour, Date, Place	Summary of Events and Information	Remarks and references to Appendices
8.3.16 Sutton Veny	Parade under Platoon Commanders 7.15am for dodging exercise. The parade was dismissed owing to frozen ground required for thawing snow from roads. 9.10am Physical Training Bayonet fighting. Battalion paraded for route march with Battalion Route taken:— No 9 CAMP on SUTTON VENY, LONGBRIDGE DEVERIL Rd — N to CROCKERTON — W to corner S of S in BUCKLERS WOOD — NE to new road at BORE HILL — S to point 400 — E through SOUTHLEIGH WOOD to No 9 CAMP. Rifle & foot inspection was carried out on return to camp. Miniature range was used by 20 men throughout the day. Bombs were cleaned.	SMF SMF SMF SMF SMF SMF
9.3.16 Sutton Veny	Parade 7.15am on Quick under Platoon Commanders for dodging. Whole Battalion 9am–9.55am marched new recruits together for training. 18 C men paraded for digging, 2.55am under Reg Sgt Major Brown. Bayonet fighting and Musketry. Hay Guard for practice (50 yds–100 yds) on open range during the morning. Miniature Range was used throughout the day by 20 men & NCOs. Bombers paraded on range & cleaned. Night piquet was carried out. Platoon Concentration march on front of HILL (B 4 1st Sheet 13.2) Tour of Observation 9pm. Cross Roads interviewed by York Hamilton line on S of 11th L in LITTLECOMBE	SMF SMF SMF SMF SMF SMF SMF
9.3.16		

Army Form C. 2118.

WAR DIARY
or
INTELLIGENCE SUMMARY.
(Erase heading not required.)

Instructions regarding War Diaries and Intelligence Summaries are contained in F.S. Regs., Part II. and the Staff Manual respectively. Title pages will be prepared in manuscript.

Hour, Date, Place	Summary of Events and Information	Remarks and references to Appendices
10.3.16. Sutton Veny	Parade 9.15am under Platoon Commanders for usual doubling exercise. 9am + 2pm trained men & recruits paraded together for training. 20 men & NCOs used the Miniature Range throughout the day. 13 men left Battalion to join 10th Prov Bttn this day. Extract from LONDON GAZETTE March 8th Cy Sgt May. R.A. Bain to be 2/Lt (on probn) Jan 14 Sergt S.A. Pattinson " " " " Nuts 29 +33 are this day declared isolated.	S.A.P. S.A.P. S.A.P. S.A.P. S.A.P.
11.3.16 "	Parade 9.15am under Platoon Commanders for usual doubling. Kit & foot inspection was carried out and shirts were washed out during the morning. Bombing class paraded in Recreation Room today.	S.A.P. S.A.P. S.A.P.
12.3.16 "	Divine Service.	Scots
13.3.16 "	Parade at 7.15 A.M. under Platoon Commanders for morning exercise and drill. 9 A.M. trained men & recruits paraded for training. Battalion paraded at 10.30 for a Route March - Route taken - Sutton Veny - Tytherington - Sutton Veny - LONGBRIDGE DEVERILL - ROOK HILL - MONKTON DEVERILL - ROOK HILL - back. 31 men joined from the 10th Provisional Bn. Major Layton (R.A.M.C.) lectured to all officers on his experiences in France.	Scots Scots Scots
14.3.16 "	Parade under Platoon Commanders for morning exercise and drill. Brigade Yachead Scheme.	Scots Scots Scots

(73989) W4141—463. 400,000. 9/14. H.&J. Ltd. Forms/C. 2118/10.

WAR DIARY
or
INTELLIGENCE SUMMARY.
(Erase heading not required.)

Army Form C. 2118.

Instructions regarding War Diaries and Intelligence Summaries are contained in F.S. Regs., Part II. and the Staff Manual respectively. Title pages will be prepared in manuscript.

Hour, Date, Place	Summary of Events and Information	Remarks and references to Appendices
10.3.16 Sutton Veny	Parade 9.15am under Platoon Commanders (to inspect clothing issued). Four Army Brand novices recruits paraded together for training. Remainder of N.C.O.s went over miniature range throughout the day. 13 men left Battalion 4 hours 1915 from Bath this day. Extract from LONDON GAZETTE March 8th. Relinquishes his 2/Lt. (on probn.) Jan. 14. Capt. & Temp.R. McBean. Sergt. S.A. Pattinson. Sergt. S.A. Pattinson. Hos 24-53 am Thos Lent postical overalls.	S&P S&P S&P S&P S&P
11.3.16 "	Parade 9.15am under Platoon Commanders for usual drill, kit inspection, an account of which was noted absent from the morning parade. Parade was formed on Relation Parade today.	S&P S&P S&P S&B
12.3.16 "	Divine Service	
13.3.16	Parade at 9.15AM under Platoon Commanders for running training exercises. 9AM route march would proceed to training Battalion paraded 10 to 10:30 for a Route march — Route taken — Sutton Veny — Heytesbury — Tytherington — Bishop's Strow — SUTTON VENY LONGBRIDGE DEVERILL — ROCK HILL — MONKTON DEVER— ILL. (exclusive of officers who ??? ??? in France.	S&B S&B S&B
14.3.16	Parade under Platoon Commanders for running exercises and Brigade Jacking School	S&B

Army Form C. 2118.

WAR DIARY
or
INTELLIGENCE SUMMARY.
(Erase heading not required.)

Instructions regarding War Diaries and Intelligence Summaries are contained in F.S. Regs., Part II and the Staff Manual respectively. Title pages will be prepared in manuscript.

Hour, Date, Place	Summary of Events and Information	Remarks and references to Appendices
15 March 1916 Sutton Veny.	Parade at 7.15 A.M. for running exercises & drill. A Court of enquiry assembled to enquire into the loss of the kit of N.co's & OO1. Lecture to Officers & N.C.O.'s on Gas attacks by Capt. Cathcart with a demonstration. Battalion paraded for training under Coy. Officers. Night Operations starting at 9.30. Lecture on Discipline to all Officers by the Brigade Major.	SWB SWB SWB Appendix B.
16 March 1916 do.	Parade at 7.15 A.M. for running exercise. The alarm sounded at 3 minutes to 9. A.M. It was in the nature of a practice alarm. Battalion paraded at 2 p.m. in accordance to programme. Party paraded under Capt. Hunter for digging. The Acts of gallantry for which 2nd Lt Anderson & 2nd Lt Glen Burn received their D.C.M.'s was published in Orders. 2nd Lt. Anderson. "for conspicuous gallantry & good services. He invariably displayed great bravery & coolness under fire.". 2nd Lt. E. Burn "for conspicuous gallantry. He was always ready to volunteer for any hazardous work & displayed great bravery & coolness on all occasions.	SWB SWB SWB
17 March 1916 do	Parade at 7.15 A.M. for running exercise. 59 men paraded under Capt. Hunter for firing two practices (10 rounds) Grouping 50+. Application 100+. Training according to programme laid down was carried out. 50 men paraded under Capt. N.A. Tulis for digging. 2nd Lt. Chisholm. 2nd Lt. Potts of the 3rd Bn. joined this Bn. to day.	SWB SWB
18 March 1916 do	Capt Grey of the 10th Bn. Lt. R Scott joined this Bn. this day. Parade at 7.15 A.M. for running exercise. Kit Inspection. Huts were washed out.	SWB SWB
19 March 1916 do	Divine Service was held for all Denominations.	SWB

WAR DIARY
or
INTELLIGENCE SUMMARY.
(Erase heading not required.)

Army Form C. 2118.

Instructions regarding War Diaries and Intelligence Summaries are contained in F.S. Regs., Part II and the Staff Manual respectively. Title pages will be prepared in manuscript.

Hour, Date, Place	Summary of Events and Information	Remarks and references to Appendices
15 March 1916 Sutton Veny	Paraded 7.15 AM for running exercise & walk out. Great difficulty experienced in assembling in time & B & D Coys of the Battalion (at present under command of Captain Ethersal with admonition. Battalion paraded for training under Coys. Officers. Right of each platoon stationed at P.S.S. lecture meeting held of Officers by the Brigade Major.	See 8 See 8 See 8 Appendix B
16 March 1916 do.	Paraded 7.15 AM for running & exercises. The Battalion assembled at 8 AM Drum & Fife sound the advance alone to programme. Battalion paraded 2 P.M. under Coy Cmdrs to programme. Smoke paraded under Capt Hunter for digging "The art of retaining the trench." D. & C. Coy under Capt Anderson & D. & Lt Peter Russ assumed the D.C.O. His men practiced in crown & cadence by Company training. Pool Lecture to N.C.O.s by Captain Inglis on "the conveyance, range, & sight rules" He continues his work to instruct the N.C.O.s as comprehensively as the time available will permit. Hours practiced.	See 8 See 8 See 8
17 March 1916 do.	Paraded 7.15 AM for running & exercises. 58 parade under Serg (name) printed under Captain Anderson two hours practice(commands) Practice Shot shooters in shower. Lectured N.C.O.s on P.S.S. Cadence was continued. Battalion pde 2 P.M. of P.S. of Co. 50 & 58 B. of K. at stand near M.G. gun.	See 8 See 8
18 March 1916 do.	Paraded 7.15 AM for running exercise. Rifle were inspected by R. & Left found the D.N. B. for today.	See 8 See 8
19 March 1916 do.	Divine Service was held for all Denominations	See 8

Army Form C. 2118.

WAR DIARY
or
INTELLIGENCE SUMMARY.
(Erase heading not required.)

Instructions regarding War Diaries and Intelligence Summaries are contained in F.S. Regs., Part II. and the Staff Manual respectively. Title pages will be prepared in manuscript.

Hour, Date, Place	Summary of Events and Information	Remarks and references to Appendices
20 March 1916 Sutton Veny.	Coy Companies paraded at 6.40 A.M. for General Musketry Course. A.B. do do 11.50 " Isolated Party paraded at 8.15 A.M. for training under 2nd Lieut. W. Andrew. Night operations were postponed owing to the wet.	S.W.B.
21 March 1916 do.	Owing to heavy rain the General Musketry Course was postponed. Companies carried on training in Huts. Capt. J.L. Duncan left for 10 days leave.	S.W.B.
22 March 1916 do.	Field Marshall Viscount French inspected the draft of 81 men who joined this Battalion on the 14th inst. He also presented the Distinguished Conduct Medal to 2nd Lieut. W. Andrew, son of 2nd Lt. Colin Burns.	S.W.B.
23 March 1916 do.	The General Musketry Course was carried on according to programme. Isolated Party paraded under Lieut. S.W.Brennan for digging.	S.W.B.
24 March 1916 do.	The General Musketry Course was carried on according to programme. The Inspector General of Infantry inspected the Companies at work on the trench Assault.	S.W.B.

Army Form C. 2118.

WAR DIARY
or
INTELLIGENCE SUMMARY.
(Erase heading not required.)

Instructions regarding War Diaries and Intelligence Summaries are contained in F.S. Regs., Part II. and the Staff Manual respectively. Title pages will be prepared in manuscript.

Hour, Date, Place	Summary of Events and Information	Remarks and references to Appendices
20 March 1916 Sutton Veny	O.C. Coy was present at 6:10 A.M. for General Rundell's Guard. A.O.S. at 11:50. Salute Party paraded at 8:15 A.M. for trooping and took to Andover. Rifle inspection was postponed owing to the wet.	S.W.O.
21 March 1916 do.	Owing to General Rundell's Guard was postponed Coy was carried on training in field. Capt. F.L. Bruce left for 10 days leave.	S.W.O.
22 March 1916 do.	Lieut. the great Viscount Sherard inspected at rest of 31 men who proved no Cordon in the Coy not yet received the Distinguished Conduct medals to which he was Emt to Audw from D. do at Cokin Rooms	S.W.O.
23 March 1916 do.	The General Inspection of Coy was carried on according to Programme. Details of M.G. posted under Lieut. Richman and Layers.	S.W.O.
24 March 1916 do.	The General Rundell, C.B.E. was carried on according to Programme. The Brig. the General of Infantry inspected the Companies at work on the Hand Grenade.	S.W.O.

(73989) W4141—463. 400,000. 9/14. H.&J.Ltd. Forms/C. 2118/10.

Army Form C. 2118.

WAR DIARY
or
INTELLIGENCE SUMMARY.
(Erase heading not required.)

Instructions regarding War Diaries and Intelligence Summaries are contained in F.S. Regs., Part II. and the Staff Manual respectively. Title pages will be prepared in manuscript.

Hour, Date, Place	Summary of Events and Information	Remarks and references to Appendices
25 March 1916 Sutton Veny	General musketry Course was carried on. Huts were cleaned & washed.	SWB
26 March 1916 do.	Divine Service for all Denominations. C.O. inspected at Huts at 11.30.	SWB
27 March 1916 do.	General musketry Course continued. Lecture to all Officers on Lewis Gun by the Brigade Machine Gun Officer.	SWB
28 March 1916 do.	Owing to bad weather Shooting was postponed. Training was carried on in Huts.	SWB
29 March 1916 do.	General musketry Course continued. Lecture to all Officers on Machine & Lewis Guns.	SWB
30 March 1916 do.	General musketry Course continued. Owing to bad state of ground, digging was cancelled.	SWB
31 March 1916 do.	Training according to program was carried on. 26 men joined this day from 1st 3/1/11 to Bn. East Sheen. Lecture to all Officers on Lewis Gun by Brigade Machine Gun Officer.	SWB SWB SWB

WAR DIARY
or
INTELLIGENCE SUMMARY.
(Erase heading not required.)

Army Form C. 2118.

Instructions regarding War Diaries and Intelligence Summaries are contained in F.S. Regs., Part II. and the Staff Manual respectively. Title pages will be prepared in manuscript.

Hour, Date, Place	Summary of Events and Information	Remarks and references to Appendices
25 March 1916 Sutton Veny	Funeral of Major Cruise was attended on 1/4 was demonstrated.	S.u.B.
26 March 1916 do.	Divine Service for all Denominations. C.O. inspected at Mr. at 11.30	S.u.B.
27 March 1916 do.	General musketry Course entered. Lecture to all officers on Lewis Gun by the Brigade Machine Gun Officer.	S.u.B.
28 March 1916 do.	Owing to bad weather, shooting was postponed. Training was carried on it [?].	S.M.
29 March 1916 do.	Supply train? Lecture was given. Lecture to all Officers on Machine & Lewis Guns.	S.u.B.
30 March 1916 do.	General musketry Course entered. Owing to bad weather, photographing the [?] for snipers etc.	S.u.B.
31 August 1916 do.	Training as usual for regiment were carried on. 2.0 p.m. paraded the day for all 3/m to 3/m East Shaw. Lecture to all Officers on Lewis Guns by the Brigade Machine Gun Officer.	S.u.B.

(73989) W4141-463. 400,000. 9/14. H.&J.Ltd. Forms/C. 2118/10.

War Diary.
of
The 2/14th Battalion London Regt.
London Scottish.

1st. April 1916 to 30th. April 1916.

Army Form C. 2118.

WAR DIARY
or
INTELLIGENCE SUMMARY.
(Erase heading not required.)

Instructions regarding War Diaries and Intelligence Summaries are contained in F.S. Regs., Part II and the Staff Manual respectively. Title pages will be prepared in manuscript.

Hour, Date, Place	Summary of Events and Information	Remarks and references to Appendices
1st April 1916. Sutton Veny.	Training according to programme. Huts were washed and blankets aired.	Scots
2nd April 1916. do.	Divine Service for all Denominations. Hut Inspection by C.O. at 11.30 A.M.	Scots
3rd April 1916. do.	Early morning hrs at 7.15 A.M. Training according to programme. Night digging cancelled.	Scots
4th April 1916. do.	Parade 7.15. Lieut. Monro attended Lewis Gunner's course of firing. Training according to programme.	Scots
5th April 1916. do.	Parade 7.15. Training according to programme. Two Cookers were sent for repair.	Scots
6th April 1916. do.	Parade 7.15. Training according to programme.	Scots
7th April 1916. do.	The Alarm sounded at 8.15, in accordance with 60th Division orders 100 dated 9th March, to go forth week.	Scots
8th April 1916. do.	Training according to programme. Laid down.	Scots
9th April 1916. do.	Divine Service for all Denominations. Hut Inspection by the C.O. at 11 A.M.	Scots
10th April 1916. do.	General Musketry Course for 2nd Early started. Training according to programme. The following equipment was drawn this day. Signalling equipment. – 1 Barr & Stroud Instrument – 16 French Stretchers – Drums & Bugles.	Scots

(73989) W4141—463. 400,000. 9/14. H.&J. Ltd. Forms/C. 2118/10.

WAR DIARY
or
INTELLIGENCE SUMMARY.
(Erase heading not required.)

Army Form C. 2118.

Hour, Date, Place	Summary of Events and Information	Remarks and references to Appendices
1st April 1916 Sutton Veny	Training according to programme. Hills were washed out between sand.	S.o.S
2nd April 1916 do.	Divine Service. Frances Dumaresa His Lordship the C.O. at 11.30 A.M.	S.o.S
3rd April 1916 do.	Early morning and 11.15 A.M. parades according to Night drying parades.	S.o.S
4th April 1916 do.	Parade 7.15 Had memo attached Specs Gunnery attended two of 3 coys. according to programme laid down.	S.o.S
5th April 1916 do.	Parade 7.15. Training according to programme. The Coys. were sent forward to prepare.	S.o.S
6th April 1916 do.	Parade 7.15. Training according to programme.	S.o.S
7th April 1916 do.	The Army acted 18/19, in accordance with 60 Division Orders No. dated 9th March to go into a week of trenches. Training according to programme laid down.	S.o.S
8th April 1916 do.	Divine Service. Parade Denomination. His Lordship the C.O. at 11 A.M.	S.o.S
9th April 1916 do.	General tidying (cause to 2nd Party Started) training according to Bylaws. The following Equipment was drawn this day. Signalling Equipment – 18 pairs Rifle, Batterel – 16 Trench Stretchers – Barre Rifle Etc.	S.o.S S.o.S

Osborne Duncan Lt. Col

WAR DIARY
or
INTELLIGENCE SUMMARY.
(Erase heading not required.)

Army Form C. 2118.

Instructions regarding War Diaries and Intelligence Summaries are contained in F.S. Regs., Part II and the Staff Manual respectively. Title pages will be prepared in manuscript.

Hour, Date, Place	Summary of Events and Information	Remarks and references to Appendices
11 April 1916 – Sutton Veny	General Musketry Course Continued. Men not shooting carried on training according to programme.	SusB
12 April 1916 do.	Work was carried on according to programme.	SusB
13 April 1916 do.	Capt. J.L. Duncan left to join the 3rd Bn. East Surrey. Work was carried on according to programme.	SusB
14 April 1916 do.	16 Binoculars & Pedometers were received this day.	SusB
15 April 1916 do.	Work was carried on according to programme.	SusB
16 April 1916 do.	All huts were thoroughly cleaned. Divine Service to all Denominations. Training as to programme.	SusB
17 April 1916 do.	General Musketry Course continued. Lieut. Mitchell returned from sick leave. Lieut. Mitchell left to join the 3rd Battalion East Surrey.	SusB
18 April 1916 do.	Training was carried on according to programme.	SusB
19 April 1916 do.	do.	SusB
20 April 1916 do.	do.	SusB
21 April 1916 do.	Divine Service to all denominations. Battalion Sports were held in the afternoon. Prizes were presented by the Brigadier's wife.	SusB
22 April 1916 do.	Training was carried on according to programme.	SusB

Army Form C. 2118.

WAR DIARY
or
INTELLIGENCE SUMMARY.
(Erase heading not required.)

Instructions regarding War Diaries and Intelligence Summaries are contained in F. S. Regs., Part II. and the Staff Manual respectively. Title pages will be prepared in manuscript.

Hour, Date, Place	Summary of Events and Information	Remarks and references to Appendices
11 April 1916 Sutton Veny	General Inspecting General Estimated. Training was generally carried out. Parade according to programme	S.of A
12 April 1916 do.	Work was carried on according to programme	S.of B
13 April 1916 do.	Capt. St. Duncan left for the 3rd Res. Battn. Training carried on according to programme. No Divisional or Brigade orders received this day	S.of B S.of A. S.of B
14 April 1916 do.	Training carried on as usual to programme	S.of A
15 April 1916 do.	All ranks were thought a period lecture as to programme	S.of B
16 April 1916 do.	Divine Service held. Demonstration but but returned from leave	S.of B
17 April 1916 do. 18 April 1916 do.	General Inspecting General returned. Got his sleeve up to .... Aug.st Patricia Rank Slare	S.of B S.of B
19 April 1916 do.	Training was carried on according to programme	S.of B
	do.	
20 April 1916 do.	do.	S.of B
21 April 1916 do.	Day Service in ate demonstrations. Battalion Sports was held in the afternoon. Programme was preceded by the Brigadier's talk	S.of B
22 April 1916 do.	Training was carried on according to programme	S.of B

Army Form C. 2118.

WAR DIARY
or
INTELLIGENCE SUMMARY.
(Erase heading not required.)

Instructions regarding War Diaries and Intelligence Summaries are contained in F.S. Regs., Part II and the Staff Manual respectively. Title pages will be prepared in manuscript.

Hour, Date, Place	Summary of Events and Information	Remarks and references to Appendices
23 April 1916 Sutton Veny	Divine Service for all Denominations	SWB
24 April 1916 do.	The Battalion moved to No. 15 Sandhill Camp, Longbridge Deverill.	SWB
25 April 1916 Longbridge Deverill	Fatigue parties proceeded to No 9 Camp, Sutton Veny to clean camp. Musketry Practice at Ground. Work commenced. Night work. Practice relief of trenches.	SWB
26 April 1916 do.	Training according to programme.	SWB
27 April 1916 do.	do.	SWB
28 April 1916 do.	Training according to programme. The alarm was sounded at 7.30. Orders were given to the Bn. to mobilize.	SWB
29 April 1916 do.	The C.O. 9 officers + 303 C.Coy Coy Platoon of A — dismissed Ireland. Lieut Murphy was O/C of details. Major Cartwright in command of the Details.	SWB
30 April 1916 do.	Maj. Cartwright in command of the rest of the Bn. 3 Platoons of A Coy B. + D. Coy. Divine Service for all denominations. Standing by Orders for an early move on Monday morning were received and cancelled later.	SWB

WAR DIARY
or
INTELLIGENCE SUMMARY.
(Erase heading not required.)

Army Form C. 2118.

Hour, Date, Place	Summary of Events and Information	Remarks and references to Appendices
23 April 1916 Sutton Veny	Divine Service for all Denominations	SVS
24 April 1916 do.	The Bn. at 8am marched to N° 15 Sandhurst Camp. Longbridge Deverill	SVS
25 April 1916 Longbridge Deverill	Fatigue parties proceeded to N° 9 Camp Suttn Veny to clean Camp. Arms Drill & Practice being general was carried out. Works with Practice reliefs of trenches "Drawing & supply to trenches."	SVS
26 April 1916 do.	do.	SVS
27 April 1916 do.		SVS
28 April 1916 do.	Training carried out as usual. The A/Adjt. was appointed as C.R.S	SVS
29 April 1916 do.	The O.C. announced 303 to be O. it at the Army Corps Gymkhana 1st May. The C.O. Officers + C.Q.M.S. nearly all played at Warminster	SVS
30 April 1916 d	Remainder rested. Less the 1/7 on account of the Strike. trg. (Church) in accordance of the head of the Bn. 3 Battns of A.Coys + A Sunnie parade dependent on Orders by monday morning were shewn + discussed etc	SVS

Forms/C. 2118/10.

War Diary
of
The 2/14th Bn. London Regt.
London Scottish.
1st. May 1916 to 31st. May 1916.

Army Form C. 2118.

WAR DIARY
or
INTELLIGENCE SUMMARY.
(Erase heading not required.)

Instructions regarding War Diaries and Intelligence Summaries are contained in F.S. Regs., Part II. and the Staff Manual respectively. Title pages will be prepared in manuscript.

Hour, Date, Place	Summary of Events and Information	Remarks and references to Appendices
1st May 1916 Longbridge Deverill	Training was carried on in Camp. Physical training Drill, Bayonet fighting & running exercise. Remainder of Battalion standing by.	SWB
2nd May 1916 do.	Running exercise Drill Bayonet fighting was carried on in Camp. General Fatigues for cleaning Camp. 7 men from the Inns of Court O.T.C. joined this day. 2nd Lt Coggin & two men proceeded to Pembroke Dock to bring back officers valises who did not proceed with Headquarters on Saturday the 29th inst.	SWB
3rd May 1916 do.	Running exercise at 7.15 A.M. Training under Company Officers 9 A.M. to 12.30. Ammunition & Iron rations were returned to Coy. Store rooms. Route march 2 p.m. to 4 p.m. Lt Coggin returned with officers valises from Neyland.	SWB
4th May 1916 do.	Running exercise at 7.15 A.M. B. Coy. in Musketry Range. Training from 9 A.M. to 12.30 p.m. under Coy officers. Training from 2 p.m. to 4 p.m. under Coy officers.	SWB
5th May 1916 do.	Running exercise at 7.15 A.M. 9 A.M to 12.30 p.m. 2 pm to 4 p.m. training under Company Officers	SWB

Army Form C. 2118.

WAR DIARY
or
INTELLIGENCE SUMMARY.
(Erase heading not required.)

Instructions regarding War Diaries and Intelligence Summaries are contained in F.S. Regs., Part II and the Staff Manual respectively. Title pages will be prepared in manuscript.

Hour, Date, Place	Summary of Events and Information	Remarks and references to Appendices
1st May 1916 Longbridge Deverill	Training was carried on in Camp. Physical training, Bayonet fighting & training several. Reminder of Battalion Standing by.	S.W.B.
2nd May 1916 do.	Running exercise when Bn. was together was carried on. Coy of men in Camp. General fatigues for clearing Camp. Drew dry rations from the Army I Corp O.T.C. proceeded to Perham Down to act as Coys of line men provided to Perham Down to asst. Brigade officers & others whom had not arrived until Saturday the 29th inst.	S.B. S.W.B.
3rd May 1916 do.	Headquarters arrived at 7.15 A.M. Training in the Coys. Officer 9 A.M. to 12.30. Ammunition & iron rations were returned to Coys. Stores. Route march 2 p.m. to 4 p.m. all Coys returned except Officers ladies for Hospital.	S.W.B.
4th May 1916 do.	Running exercise at 7.15 A.M. to B Coy in Hammerth. Rage. Training from 9 A.M. to 12.30 p.m. under Coy officers. Training from 2 p.m. to 4 p.m. under Coy officers.	S.W.B.
5th May 1916 do.	Running exercise at 7.15 A.M. 9 A.M. to 12.30 p.m. 2 p.m. to 4 p.m. training under Company officers.	S.W.B.

signature

Army Form C. 2118.

WAR DIARY
or
INTELLIGENCE SUMMARY.
(Erase heading not required.)

Instructions regarding War Diaries and Intelligence Summaries are contained in F.S. Regs., Part II. and the Staff Manual respectively. Title pages will be prepared in manuscript.

Hour, Date, Place	Summary of Events and Information	Remarks and references to Appendices
6th May 1916 - Longbridge - Deverill	Inspection of the Camp by the Officer Commanding the Details of the 179th Infantry Brigade. Instants the Divisional Sports took place.	SWB
7th May 1916 - do.	Divine Service for all Denominations. Inspection of the Camp by the C.O. at 11 A.M.	SWB
8th May 1916 - do.	General Musketry Course for the details who have not fired. Training under Company officers for rest of Battalion.	SWB
9th May 1916 - do.	G.M.C. continued. Training under Coy Officers	SWB
10th May 1916 - do.	G.M.C. continued. Route march by the rest of the Battⁿ.	SWB
11th May 1916 - do.	G.M.C. continued. Training under Coy Officers	SWB
12th May 1916 - do.	G.M.C. for Party finished. Training under Coy Officers	SWB
13th May 1916 - do.	Headquarters Staff of the Battalion returned from Ireland arriving Warminster 7 A.M. Transport arrived Warminster 4.20 p.m.	SWB
14th May 1916 - do.	Divine Service for all Denominations. Inspection by the Commanding Officer at 12 Noon for kit of Huts.	SWB R.B. [signature] Lt Col

(73989) W4141—463. 400,000. 9/14. H.&J.Ltd. Forms/C. 2118/10.

Army Form C. 2118.

WAR DIARY
or
INTELLIGENCE SUMMARY.
(Erase heading not required.)

Instructions regarding War Diaries and Intelligence Summaries are contained in F.S. Regs., Part II. and the Staff Manual respectively. Title pages will be prepared in manuscript.

Hour, Date, Place	Summary of Events and Information	Remarks and references to Appendices
6th May 1916. Longbridge Deverill	Inspection of the Camp by the Officer Commanding the Details of the 179th Infantry Brigade and also the Divisional Sports took place.	SWB
7th May 1916. do	Divine Service for the Denominations. Inspection of the Camp by the C.O. at 11 A.M.	SWB
8th May 1916. do	General musketry Course for the details who have not fired, and ordinary Company training to rest of Batt.	SWB
9th May 1916. do	do & & continued. Training under Coy Officers.	SWB
10th May 1916. d	do & & continued. Battle march by the rest of the Battn.	SWB
11th May 1916. d	do & & continued. Training under Coy Officers.	SWB
12th May 1916. d	The C.O. & Party proceeded to Warminster to inspect Hutments from 4.30 p.m.	SWB
13th May 1916. d	Headquarters Staff of the Battalion returned from Warminster 7 A.M.	SWB
14th May 1916. d	Divine Service for all Denominations. Inspection by the Commanding Officer at 12 Noon to of Huts.	SWB

(P. Llewelyn) C.O.

Army Form C. 2118.

WAR DIARY
or
INTELLIGENCE SUMMARY.
(Erase heading not required.)

Instructions regarding War Diaries and Intelligence Summaries are contained in F.S. Regs., Part II and the Staff Manual respectively. Title pages will be prepared in manuscript.

Hour, Date, Place	Summary of Events and Information	Remarks and references to Appendices
LONGBRIDGE DEVERILL 15 MAY 1916	Strong as first strike parade for Kit Inspection – Companies practised the attack during the afternoon.	SWS
do. 16 May 1916.	Parade 9 A.M. under the C.O. attack practice – mess tin cooking – Night Work – Parade 8 p.m.	SWS
do 17 May 1916.	Morning run at 7.15 A.M. Battalion Route march. Mess tin cooking	SWS
do 18 May 1916.	Morning run at 7.15 A.M. Close Order Drill. Training under Company Officers.	SWS
d 19 May 1916.	Morning run at 7.15 A.M. Battalion in the trenches. Mess tin cooking.	SWS
do 20 May 1916.	Close Order Drill. Kit, Boot & Feet Inspection. All Huts washed out. Blankets aired.	SWS
do 21 May 1916	Training in Camp. Inspection Gas masks, feet S.W. Browne by Int. Officer.	SWS
do 22 May 1916	~~Parade 7.15 A.M. under Platoon Commanders. Dress In Canvas kit Shorts.~~	~~SWS~~
do 23 May 1916	~~Inspection Billets & Stores.~~	~~SWS~~
do 21 May 1916	Divine Service for all Denominations. Inspection of Huts by the C.O. at 11.30 A.M.	SWS

Donna Lt. Col.

WAR DIARY
or
INTELLIGENCE SUMMARY.
(Erase heading not required.)

Army Form C. 2118.

Instructions regarding War Diaries and Intelligence Summaries are contained in F. S. Regs., Part II and the Staff Manual respectively. Title pages will be prepared in manuscript.

Hour, Date, Place	Summary of Events and Information	Remarks and references to Appendices
LONGBRIDGE DEVERILL 15 May 1916.	Strong aggressive advance to full inspection. Companies finished and the Officers away during the afternoon	SWB
do. 16 May 1916.	Parade 9 A.M. under the C.O. Other Parades near the Cooking. Night work. Parades 5pm	SWB
do. 17 May 1916.	Training at 7.15 A.M. D.H. & on Rifle meets the 7 Coys. from 4 to 7.15 A.M. Close Order Drill. Training with Company Officers	SWB
do. 18 May 1916.		SWB
do. 19 May 1916.	Training. Rev. at 7.15 A.M. Battalion in the trenches. Mess & Cookings	SWB
do. 20 May 1916.	Close Order Drill. Kit, Foot & Feet Inspection all Huts inspected. Blankets aired.	SWB
do. 21 May 1916.	Church Parade. Attended by the whole Battn. Second half of Holiday given to the Coys by the CO	SWB
do. 22 May 1916.		SWB
do.		
do. 23 May 1916.	Brigade Sports & presentation of Inspection of Hut by R.C.O. at 11.30 A.M.	SWB

[signature]

Army Form C. 2118.

WAR DIARY
or
INTELLIGENCE SUMMARY.
(Erase heading not required.)

Instructions regarding War Diaries and Intelligence Summaries are contained in F.S. Regs. Part II and the Staff Manual respectively. Title pages will be prepared in manuscript.

Hour, Date, Place	Summary of Events and Information	Remarks and references to Appendices
LONGBRIDGE DEVERILL 22 May 1916	Morning run at 7.15 A.M. Training was carried on in Camp.	S.W.B.
23 May 1916 do.	Morning run at 7.15 A.M. Transport Cooking by Battalion during Out Post Practice.	S.W.B.
24 May 1916 do.	Divisional Route march - Parade 7.20 A.M.	S.W.B.
25 May 1916 do.	Paraded. Parade 7.30 for Night Work. Trench Schemes. Parade under Coy Officers at 11 A.M. & 2 P.M.	S.W.B.
26 May 1916 do.	Parade 6.30 for Divisional exercise.	S.W.B.
27 May 1916 do.	Parade 7.15 A.M. Boot Inspection - Kits washed. Close Order Drill.	S.W.B.
28 May 1916 do.	Divine Service for all Denominations. Kit Inspection.	S.W.B.
29 May 1916 do.	Field firing for A. & B. Coys. C. & D. training under Coy. Officers.	S.W.B.
30 May 1916 do.	Rehearsal for Review by King on 31st inst. 5 Pipers & 8 Drummers lent by 2nd Bn arrived from London	S.W.B.
31 May 1916 do.	Inspection by H.M. King George.	S.W.B.

Army Form C. 2118.

WAR DIARY
or
INTELLIGENCE SUMMARY.
(Erase heading not required.)

Instructions regarding War Diaries and Intelligence Summaries are contained in F.S. Regs., Part II and the Staff Manual respectively. Title pages will be prepared in manuscript.

Hour, Date, Place	Summary of Events and Information	Remarks and references to Appendices
LONGBRIDGE DEVERILL 22 May 1916	Reveille sounded at 7.15 A.M. Trainings as carried on in Camp.	S.W.B.
23 May 1916 do.	Reveille sounded at 7.15 A.M. and the Coy's by Battalion did Out Post Practice.	R.W.B.
24 May 1916 do.	Divisional Sports took part Parade 10 A.M.	S.W.B
25 May 1916 do.	Reveille. Parade 7.30 for Night Wade Guard Scheme. Parade under Coy 11oc at 11 A.M & 2 P.m.	S.W.B
26 May 1916 do.	Parade 6.30 for Divisional exercise	S.W.B
27 May 1916 do.	Parade 7.15 A.M Boot Inspection. Kits marked. Close Order Drill.	S.W.B.
28 May 1916 do.	Divine Service for all Denominations. Kit Inspection.	S.W.B
29 May 1916 do.	Field Firing for A & B Coys. C & D Company 11oc. Officers.	S.W.B.
30 May 1916 do.	Returned to Review by King. 3 Bn at 5 from 1st Brigading Reviewed by H.M. Bn arrived from London	S.W.B
31 May 1916 d.	Inspected by H.M. King George.	S.W.B (signature)

War Diary
of the
2/14th Bn. London Regt.
London Scottish
from
1st June 1916 to 20th June 1916.

Army Form C. 2118.

WAR DIARY
or
INTELLIGENCE SUMMARY.
(Erase heading not required.)

Instructions regarding War Diaries and Intelligence Summaries are contained in F.S. Regs., Part II and the Staff Manual respectively. Title pages will be prepared in manuscript.

Hour, Date, Place	Summary of Events and Information	Remarks and references to Appendices
1 June 1916 LONGBRIDGE DEVERILL	⅓ of Battalion proceeded on 4 days leave. Remainder training under Company Officers.	SWB
2 June 1916 do.	Morning Parade 7.15 A.M. Training under Company Officers 9 A.M. to 12.30 P.M. 2 P.M. to 4.15 P.M.	SWB
3 June 1916 do.	Training under Company Officers. Huts washed out.	SWB
4 June 1916 do.	Divine Service for all Denominations. Hut Inspection at 11.30 A.M. 1st leave party returned.	SWB
5 June 1916 do.	2nd leave party left. Training for remainder of Battalion under Coy. arrangements.	SWB
6 June 1916 do.	7.15 A.M. early morning Parade. Training under Coy. arrangements. Draft of 77 men joined us today from the Reserve Bn.	SWB
7 June 1916 do.	7.15 A.M. early morning Parade. Battalion Route March. Musketry Classes for Draft.	SWB
8 June 1916 do.	7.15 A.M. morning Parade. Training under Company arrangements.	SWB
9 June 1916 do.	7.15 A.M. morning Parade. Training under Company arrangements.	SWB

(73989) W4141—463. 400,000. 9/14. H.&J.,Ltd. Forms/C. 2118/10.

WAR DIARY
or
INTELLIGENCE SUMMARY.
(Erase heading not required.)

Army Form C. 2118.

Instructions regarding War Diaries and Intelligence Summaries are contained in F.S. Regs., Part II and the Staff Manual respectively. Title pages will be prepared in manuscript.

Hour, Date, Place	Summary of Events and Information	Remarks and references to Appendices
1 June 1916 LONGBRIDGE DEVERILL	8.15 AM the Battalion on today's route. Remainder training under Company Officers	S.W.B.
2 June 1916 do.	Wiring Party 15 AM Remainder under Co. Officers 9 AM to 2.30 PM 2 PM to 4 PM	S.W.B.
3 June 1916 do.	Training under Company Officers. Hut inspection.	S.W.B.
4 June 1916 do.	Divine Service at 10 AM and in the evening Battalion photograph at 11.30 AM	S.W.B.
5 June 1916 do.	3 leave party returned	S.W.B.
	2nd leave party left. Fife drums & sphere moved off 12.45 to Colham	S.W.B.
6 June 1916 do.	Fire for area S.W.B.	S.W.B.
7 June 1916 do.	7.15 AM and Winding Parade leaving side Co. inspect. Draft of 17 men ed ready from the Reserve Bn.	S.W.B.
	7.15 AM antic onehow sides Battalion Field kick	S.W.B.
8 June 1916 do.	Training Cleanis the Draft	S.W.B.
	7.15 AM. morning Parade. Remainder under Company arrangements.	S.W.B.
9 June 1916 do.	7.15 AM. morning Parade. Remainder under Company arrangements.	S.W.B.

Army Form C. 2118.

WAR DIARY
or
INTELLIGENCE SUMMARY.
(Erase heading not required.)

Instructions regarding War Diaries and Intelligence Summaries are contained in F.S. Regs., Part II and the Staff Manual respectively. Title pages will be prepared in manuscript.

Hour, Date, Place	Summary of Events and Information	Remarks and references to Appendices
10 June 1916 LONGBRIDGE DEVERILL	Parade 7.15 A.M. for running. Companies under Coy. Officers 9 - 12. Huts washed out. Blankets shaken.	SW13
11 June 1916 do.	Divine Service for all Denominations. Hut Inspection by C.O. at 11.30. Men of the draft proceeded on leave until Tuesday night 5	SW13 SW13
12 June 1916 do.	Parade 7.15 A.M. for running. Firing in trenches on ground allotted to Battalion. Issue of Balmorals, Overseas Boots & Kilt aprons.	SW13 SW13
13 June 1916. do.	Parade 7.15 A.M. for running. Filling in Trenches. Remainder of Battalion under Company arrangements.	SW13
14 June 1916 do.	Parade 7.15 A.M. for running. Final G.M.C. commanded. Companies under Coy. Commanders 9 A.M. to 5 P.M. Extract from London Gazette dated 2.6.16. 2nd Lt. Jampman Capt. H.C. Sparks 1/14 Bn. London Regt. (T.F.) Awarded the Distinguished Conduct Medal. 2871. Coy. Sergt. Maj. A.P. Bell. 1/14th Bn. London Regt. (T.F.) Awarded the Military Medal. 2241 Sergt. J.H. Spencer 1/14 Bn. London Regt. (T.F.)	SW13 SW13 SW13 SW13
15 June 1916 do.	Parade 7.15 A.M. for running. Parade on strong parade. Kit Inspection. Issue of Gas Helmets.	SW13 SW13
16 June 1916 do.	Parade 7.15 A.M. for running. Route march for A.C.& D. Coys. B Coy. 10 A.M. C. Coy 2.30 P.M. Medical Inspection of B Coy.	SW13 SW13

WAR DIARY
or
INTELLIGENCE SUMMARY.
(Erase heading not required.)

Army Form C. 2118.

Instructions regarding War Diaries and Intelligence Summaries are contained in F.S. Regs., Part II. and the Staff Manual respectively. Title pages will be prepared in manuscript.

Hour, Date, Place	Summary of Events and Information	Remarks and references to Appendices
10 June 1916 LONGBRIDGE DEVERILL	Parade 7.15 A.M. for running Companies under Coy Officers 9-12. Huts washed out. Blankets stacked out.	SoS
11 June 1916 do.	Divine Service. Parade Denominations. Hot dispute. R.C.O at 9.30. None of the men's presented a have until Wednesday.	SoS SoS
12 June 1916 do.	Parade 7.15 A.M. for running & ¾ sw Jumping & ground attack. Battalion same of afternoon. exercise. Bomb & M.W. aping.	SoS
13 June 1916 do.	Parade 7.15 A.M. for running village attacks (similar to Battalion man Company mangement).	SoS
14 June 1916 do.	Parade 7.15 A.M. for running. Shoot of N.C.O. Group[?] and Coy. Commanders 9 A.M. 1.5 P.M. Batl shoot Gen Butler dies 2.615 2 Lt Vere Green Capt T.C. Sprigg & N.B. Jude Regt award I. Appointed 2.Lt Batley Staff Coy A hidall. 2nd Lt Coy[?] Any A Bde. 2nd Lt Lutz Inst (TT). Ball & Leathed Machel. 2nd Lt Sing I gm Squadd Batt Int Ind. Sing (TF).	SoS SoS SoS SoS SoS SoS
15 June 1916 do.	Parade 7.15 A.M. for running Sword in Slings parade & Kit Inspect Issue of Gas Helmets.	SoS
16 June 1916 do.	Parade 7.15 A.M. gm. running. Rout march for A, C & D Coys. E Coy 10 A.M. Medical Inspection of B Coy 10 A.M. E Coy 2.30 P.M.	SoS SoS

Army Form C. 2118.

WAR DIARY
or
INTELLIGENCE SUMMARY.
(Erase heading not required.)

Instructions regarding War Diaries and Intelligence Summaries are contained in F.S. Regs., Part II and the Staff Manual respectively. Title pages will be prepared in manuscript.

Hour, Date, Place	Summary of Events and Information	Remarks and references to Appendices
17 June 1916 LONGBRIDGE DEVERILL	Early morning Parade 7.15 A.m. A.T.B. Coy's paraded 9 A.m. for Route march. 3. Coy paraded 10. A.m. for medical Inspection. Lieut. B. Jenkins to be temporary Capt. 2/Lt R. H. Robertson to be Lieutenant (temporary) London Gazette.	SWB SWB
18 June 1916 do.	17 June 1916. Divine Service for all Denominations. All huts were scrubbed out with Creosote.	SWB
19 June 1916 do.	All Officers, Pipers & those who carry revolvers fired 5.0 rounds this day. Inspection by Platoons for Deficiencies.	SWB SWB
20 June 1916 do.	Companies under Company Commanders 9 A.M. to 12 Noon. Strong as possible Parade 3 P.M. them to be dressed as for Overseas.	SWB SWB

[signature]

WAR DIARY
or
INTELLIGENCE SUMMARY.
(Erase heading not required.)

Army Form C. 2118.

Instructions regarding War Diaries and Intelligence Summaries are contained in F.S. Regs., Part II and the Staff Manual respectively. Title pages will be prepared in manuscript.

Hour, Date, Place	Summary of Events and Information	Remarks and references to Appendices
17 June 1916 LONGBRIDGE DEVERILL	Battalion parade 7.15 A.M. The Coys paraded 9 A.M. for Route march. Bn paraded 10 A.M. for Medical Inspection. Lieut. B. Jolly is to be leaving Capt. 2nd H.R. & reported to 2nd Leinster (temporary) [vide Gazette 17 June 1916]	See B See B
18 June 1916 do.	Divine service & examination of all horses saddles &c with escort	See B
19 June 1916 do.	All officers & N.C.Os were at examination and so noted the day reported by Platoons to Refreshers	See B See B
20 June 1916 do.	Capt. I. Smith (Comd'g 16 Canadians 9 A.M. till 12 Noon) Strong parade paraded from 3 P.M. men 6 be drilled in formation for Inverness	See B See A

[signature]

WAR DIARY or INTELLIGENCE SUMMARY

Army Form C. 2118

(Erase heading not required.)

Instructions regarding War Diaries and Intelligence Summaries are contained in F.S. Regs., Part II. and the Staff Manual respectively. Title Pages will be prepared in manuscript.

[Stamp: LONDON REGT. CHESHIRE — 1 JUL. 1916 — LONDON SCOTTISH]

Place	Date	Hour	Summary of Events and Information	Remarks and references to Appendices
LONGBRIDGE DEVERILL	14/6/1916		Order of embarkation	1 Order of embarkation
"	18/6/1916		Train orders	2 Train orders
"	21/6/1916	9.30	HQ. A & B Coys under Lt Col ROBERT DUNSMORE handed at 9.30 AM & entrained at WARMINSTER for SOUTHAMPTON at 11.35 AM	
"		10.45	C & D Coys under Major H. CARTWRIGHT paraded at 10.45 AM & entrained at WARMINSTER for SOUTHAMPTON at 1.15 PM	
SOUTHAMPTON		5.30	sailed from SOUTHAMPTON for HAVRE on LA MARGUERITE arrived HAVRE	
HAVRE	22/6/16	1.30 AM	landed at 7 AM — proceeded to No 5 REST CAMP	
	23/6/16	8 AM	Left Rest Camp. HQ A B & D Coys under Lt Col R. DUNSMORE & entrained to LILLERS at BUNSVILLE	
BUNSVILLE		11.30	PETIT HOUVIN arrived there 4 AM 24/6/16 marched to LILLES at BUNSVILLE C Coy Major A. BLAKIE left Rest Camp at 11.30 — arrived at 1.30 marched to BUNEVILLE	
	24/6/16	12 noon	BUNEVILLE 9 AM moved to AVERDOINGT into billets here Company marched to AVERDOINGT into billets	
AVERDOINGT	28/6/16	1 pm	moved by route march to MAROEUIL arrived 10 PM went into billets	3 Line orders
MAROEUIL	29/6/16		Rested 13 officers 535 o.r. moved to ABRI CENTRALE, ANZIN	
	30/6/16	6 AM	9 AUXRIE TR. on mining fatigue Lt W. ANDERSON 12 other ranks (personnel for Light Trench Mortar Battery proceeded to T.M. School	

1875. Wt. W593/826 1,000,000 4/15 J.B.C. & A. A.D.S.S./Forms/C. 2118.

179/60

CONFIDENTIAL. Vol 2

WAR DIARY

of

2/14th. Bn. London Regt.
(London Scottish)

From :- 1/7/16   To :- 31/7/16

VOLUME No 4

Army Form C.

WAR DIARY
or
INTELLIGENCE SUMMARY
(Erase heading not required.)

2/4 BT London Regt

Instructions regarding War Diaries and Intelligence Summaries are contained in F.S. Regs., Part II. and the Staff Manual respectively. Title Pages will be prepared in manuscript.

Place	Date	Hour	Summary of Events and Information	Remarks and references to Appendices
MAROEUIL	1 July 1917		B.Wks Mining fatigue parties (6 Tg men) working in front line & billets at AUXRIETZ ABRI CENTRALE & ANZIN	
"	2 July		ditto	
"	3 July		ditto	
"	4 July		ditto	
"	5 July		Mining fatigue parties relieved by parties from 2/16 LONDR moved to billets at ECOIVRES. BN HQ & 9th & 10th stores remain at MAROEUIL – remainder of BN move to billets at ECOIVRES	
ECOIVRES	6 July 1917		Moved to trenches to take over for 6 days instruction with 1/4 Gordon HIGHRS	
TRENCHES	7 July		In trenches 2nd Lt A CECIL WILSON wounded 1 Sgt killed - Lt wounded	
"	8 July		In trenches 2nd Lt A CECIL WILSON died of wounds 8 July 1916	
"	9 July		In trenches 2 Coys in firing line 2 Coys in Bde reserve	
"	10 July		In trenches Lt Col T MACEWEN 2nd Lts J. KING, C.G. MITCHELL joined	
ditto			4th CAMEROH HIGHRS (T.F.)	
"	11 July		In trenches 2 COYS in firing line 2 Coys in reserve	
"	12 July		In trenches 2 Coys in firing line 2 Coys in reserve casualties 1 K in 4th G.H. 4 Coys firing line 2 Coys 216th L.R.	
"	13 July		In trenches Relieved by G.H.Q. reserve Centre 1. Killed one wounded three	
			output 1 Coy 2/16 GR	

Army Form C.2118

WAR DIARY or INTELLIGENCE SUMMARY

(Erase heading not required.)

2/14 Bn London Regt

Place	Date	Hour	Summary of Events and Information	Remarks and references to Appendices
IN TRENCHES	14/7/16		In addition to yesterday casualties { 4 wounded / killed 2nd Lt W.B. FALCONER Cameron HIGHRS (T.F.) joined	
"	15/7/16		Relieved in firing line by 2/15 BN L.R. 3 Coys outpost 1 Bayonne wounded 2nd Lt A.C. CHISHOLM 1 man. JOINED 2nd Lt W.J. BETHUNE T.T. CAMERON. G. STILL. O.H. GOSSIP. A. MACDOUGALL. J. TOCHER from 4th Cameron Highrs	
"	16/7/16		No yesterday casualties 2 o.r. joined 2nd Lt W.T. BROWN 4th CAMERONS T.F.	
"	17/7/16		as yesterday	
"	18/7/16		in trenches	
"	19/7/16		in trenches a.o on 17.7.16 Relieved 4 Coys in outpost + Coy out in Sufford Reserve noticed 4 Coy 2/15 BN L.R. in firing line casualties 1 wt. Lt W.T. BETHUNE 5 others ranks wounded 4	
"	20/7/16		in trenches KILLED 3. wounded 4	
"	21/7/16		in trenches wounded 1	
"	22/7/16		in trenches Died of wounds 2 Lt A.T. POWELL CAMERON HIGHRS (T.F.) wounded 1	
"	23/7/16		in trenches KILLED 1 wounded 8.	
"	24/7/16		in trenches no casualties	
"	25/7/16		in trenches no casualties	

Army Form C. 2

WAR DIARY
or
INTELLIGENCE SUMMARY 2/14 Bn London Regt
(Erase heading not required.)

Instructions regarding War Diaries and Intelligence Summaries are contained in F. S. Regs., Part II. and the Staff Manual respectively. Title Pages will be prepared in manuscript.

Place	Date	Hour	Summary of Events and Information	Remarks and references to Appendices
26/1/16	27/1/16 28/1/16 29/1/16 30/1/16 31/1/16		In the trenches Bn Relieved about 2 pm - proceeded to rest huts in BRAY In rest huts at BRAY	

[signature]
Lt. Colonel
Comdg 2/14 Bn. Lon. Regt.
(London Scottish)

2ᵈ Hudson Section
July 16

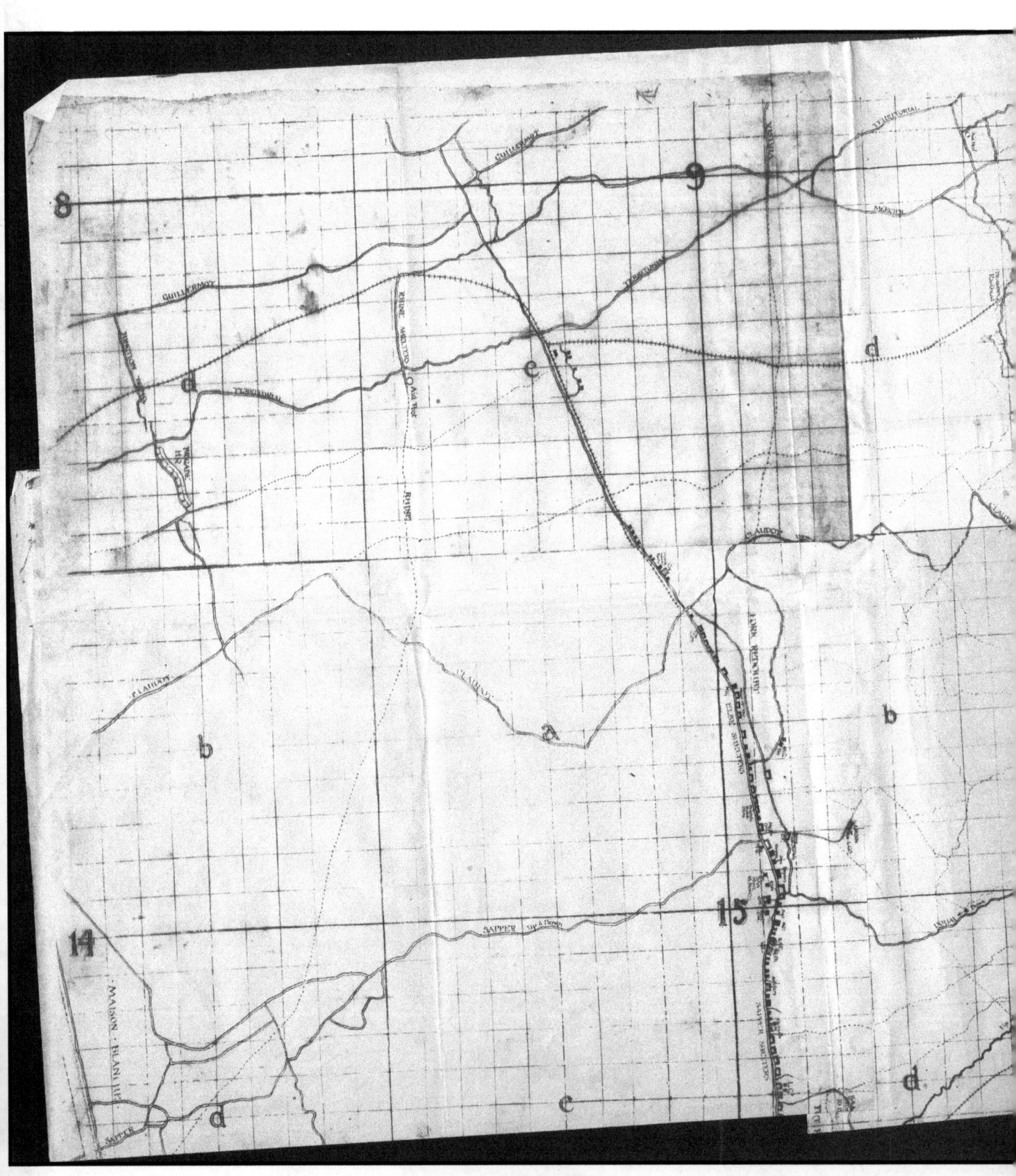

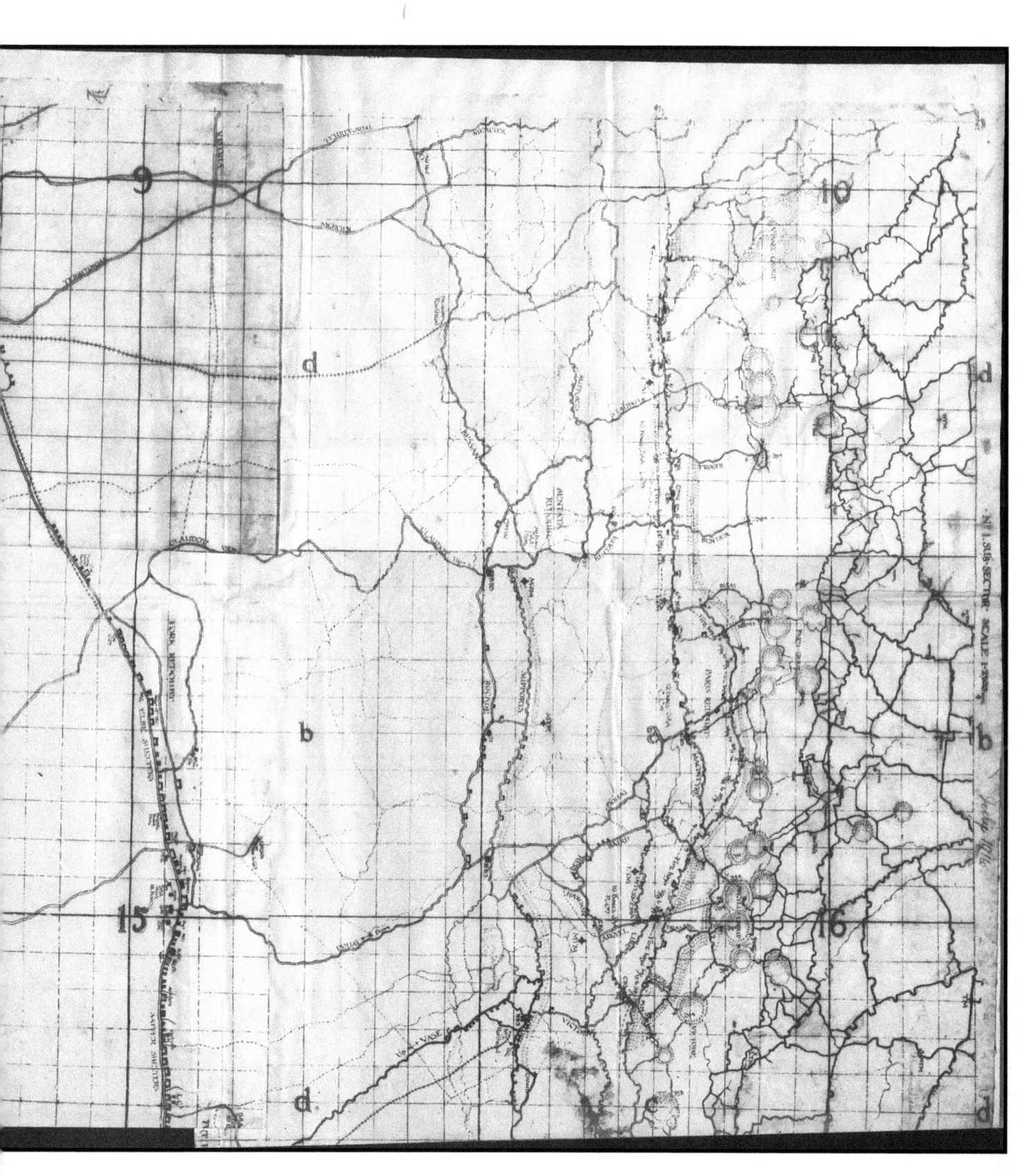

2/ London Scottish
July 1916

2° London Scottish
July '16

CONFIDENTIAL.

War Diary

of

2/14th. Bn. London Regt.
(London Scottish.)

Vol II

From:- 1/8/16   To:- 31/8/16

WAR DIARY or INTELLIGENCE SUMMARY
Army Form C. 2118

2/14 Bn London Regt
London Scottish

Place	Date	Hour	Summary of Events and Information	Remarks and references to Appendices
BRAY	1 Aug 1916		In rest billets	
"	2 Aug 1916		In rest billets	
"	3 Aug 1916		In rest billets	
"	4 Aug 1916		Moved to trenches at 2 AM relieving 2/15 LOND R in Firing Line / Coy in Support	
	5 Aug 1916		wounded Lt C. WALLIS 3 other ranks	
	6 Aug 1916		In trenches casualties 3 other ranks wounded Lt Col T. DUNSMORE wounded	
	7 Aug 1916		In trenches no casualties	
			In trenches casualties 2 wounded 2nd Lt W.J. BETHUNE 4th CAMERONS joined	
			other wounded 2nd Lt E. McLEOD & F.E. JONES 2/14 LOND R joined	
	8 Aug 1916		In trenches	
	9 Aug 1916		In trenches casualty 1 wounded	
	10 Aug 1916		In trenches casualty 1 wounded 2nd Lt D.W. BLOW 4th CAMERONS joined	
	11 Aug 1916		In trenches	
	12 Aug 1916		Relieved in firing line trenches by 2/15 LOND R. Coys moved respectively to Reserve in "CENTRE" SUPPORT and RESERVE in "CENTRE"	
	13 Aug 1916		In trenches Lt C.L. WATSON joined	
	14 Aug 1916		In trenches casualty wounded 2nd Lt F. WILSON	
	15 Aug 1916		In trenches casualty wounded one	
	16 Aug 1916		In trenches	
	17 Aug 1916		In trenches casualty wounded one	

W. Cartwright Major

Army Form C.2118

WAR DIARY
or
INTELLIGENCE SUMMARY

(Erase heading not required.)

2/14 BTT London Regt
London Scottish

Instructions regarding War Diaries and Intelligence Summaries are contained in F.S. Regs., Part II. and the Staff Manual respectively. Title Pages will be prepared in manuscript.

Place	Date	Hour	Summary of Events and Information	Remarks and references to Appendices
	18/8/16		In the trenches	
	19/8/16		In the trenches	
	20/8/16		Entrenches, delivered 2/15 BN LR in front line and left outpost	
			line. 3 wounded. Joined from England 2nd Lt. C. TENNANT and 43 other ranks	
	21/8/16		In the trenches. casualties, 3 wounded	
	22/8/16		In the trenches casualties four wounded	
	23/8/16		In the trenches casualties four wounded	
	24/8/16		In the trenches	
	25/8/16		In the trenches casualties killed 1, wounded 1	
	25/26/8/16		Raid on enemy trenches carried out by 2 L.O. under Lt. T. DD? McLean and 2/Lt OH G&S 1P 4th CATTERONS attached. Party remained out from 10.30pm to 2.15AM and all returned safely. No identification were recovered	
	26/8/16		Relieved in trenches by 1/15 BN LR - moved to rest billets in BRAY	
	27/8/16		Rest Billets BRAY	
	28/8/16		Rest Billets BRAY	
	29/8/16		Rest Billets BRAY	
	30/8/16		Rest Billets BRAY	
	31/8/16		REST BILLETS BRAY	

1875 Wt. W593/826 1,000,000 4/15 J.B.C. & A. A.D.S.S./Forms/C. 2118.

Vol 4

CONFIDENTIAL

WAR DIARY

OF

2/14TH BN LONDON REGT.
(LONDON SCOTTISH)

FROM :- 1/9/16   TO :- 30/9/16

Army Form C. 2118

WAR DIARY
or
INTELLIGENCE SUMMARY

2/14 BN LONDON REGT
LONDON SCOTTISH

(Erase heading not required.)

Instructions regarding War Diaries and Intelligence Summaries are contained in F. S. Regs., Part II. and the Staff Manual respectively. Title Pages will be prepared in manuscript.

Place	Date	Hour	Summary of Events and Information	Remarks and references to Appendices
	1 Sept 1916		Left BRAY at 2 AM relieved 2/15 BN LR in hat line dugout casualties killed 1 wounded 1	
	2 Sept 1916		In the trenches Lt. Col. T. L. OGILBY joined and assumed command. casualties wounded 1	
	3 Sept 1916		In trenches casualties wounded 2	
	4 Sept 1916		In trenches. Draft 50 o.n. joined at Rear Hdqtrs casualties nil	
	5 Sept 1916		In trenches. Enemy mine blown in front of left F.L. Coy casualties 4 killed 18 wounded	
	6 Sept 1916		In trenches relieved in FIRING LINE by 2/15th BN moved to left support and Reserve Centre I LEFT SUPPORT and RESERVE CENTRE II 1 Coy in each	
	7 Sept 1916		In trenches as above	
	8 Sept 1916		In trenches as above	
	9 Sept 1916		In trenches as above casualties two wounded	
	10 Sept 1916		In trenches as above	
	11 Sept 1916		In trenches as above	
	12 Sept 1916		In trenches as above	
	13 Sept 1916		In trenches relieved by 2/15 BN LR in Firing Line.	

M. Wyllie
Lt Col 2/14 BN LONDON R

WAR DIARY
or
INTELLIGENCE SUMMARY
(Erase heading not required.)

Army Form C. 2118

2/14 BN LONDON REGT
LONDON SCOTTISH

Place	Date	Hour	Summary of Events and Information	Remarks and references to Appendices
	14 Sept 1916		In the trenches 4 wounded 1 killed	
	15 Sept 1916		In the trenches casualties 1 killed, wounded three	
	16 Sept 1916		In the trenches casualties 1 killed, 1 wounded from	
	17 Sept 1916		In the trenches casualties, wounded 4.	
	18 Sept 1916		In the trenches casualties nil	
	19 Sept 1916		Relieved by 2/15 Bn Londn Regt & returned to REST BILLETS	
BRAY				
	20 Sept 1916		Rest Billets in BRAY	
	21 Sept 1916		Rest Billets in BRAY	
	22 Sept 1916		Rest " in BRAY	
	23 Sept 1916		Rest " " BRAY	
	24 Sept 1916		Rest Billets BRAY	
	25 Sept 1916		Relieved the 1/15 BN L.R. in the trenches	
	26 Sept 1916		In the trenches dealt 100.n SOMME	
	27 Sept 1916		casualties wounded Lt T.&C COREIN. 3.O.R. slight 1st duty for	
	28 Sept 1916		In the trenches casualties nil.	
	29 Sept 1916		In the trenches casualties 3.0.n. wounded	
	30 Sept 1916		In the trenches A raid on enemy front line trench carried out by 2/Lt T.J.O MACLAGAN & 2/Lt W.J.BETHUNE and 45 O.R. at 2.15 AM this morning the German trenches were entered several enemy were killed and 5 prisoners were taken. Casualties 1 killed 3 missing 6 wounded	M Wyllie Lt Col 2/14 BN L.R.

2/Lt C TENNANT and 11 O.R. still as covering party

Secret

Vol 5

WAR DIARY
of
2/14th Batt. London Regiment

from 1st October 1916 - to 31st October 1916.

Army Form C. 2118

WAR DIARY
or
INTELLIGENCE SUMMARY

2/14 LOND R

(Erase heading not required.)

Place	Date	Hour	Summary of Events and Information	Remarks and references to Appendices

WAR DIARY
or
INTELLIGENCE SUMMARY

Army Form C. 2118

1/14 LOND R

(Erase heading not required.)

Place	Date	Hour	Summary of Events and Information	Remarks and references to Appendices

CONFIDENTIAL.

2/14th Bt. Battalion London Regt
(London Scottish)

WAR DIARY.

November 1st. 1916.

Condensed —
Finished.

Army Form C. 2118

WAR DIARY
or
INTELLIGENCE SUMMARY 2/14 LOND R

(Erase heading not required.)

Place	Date	Hour	Summary of Events and Information	Remarks and references to Appendices
MONTIGNY	1/11/16		In Billets. Training	
"	2/11/16		In Billets. Training	
"	3/11/16		Marched to BUIGNY L'ABBÉ 14 miles	
BUIGNY	4/11/16		In Billets training	
"	5/11/16		Billets	
"	6/11/16		Billets. Bathing	
"	7/11/16		Billets. training	
"	8/11/16		Billets. training	
"	9/11/16		Billets	
"	10/11/16		Billets	
"	11/11/16		Billets. draft 59 o.r. joined	
"	12/11/16		Billets	
"	13/11/16		Billets	
"	14/11/16		Billets	
"	15/11/16		Marched 10½m. en route march 10 miles to LONGPRÉ Journeyed by train to MARSEILLES	
"	16/11/16		Arrived MARSEILLES and proceeded to MOUSSOT CAMP	
"	20/11/16		In Camp – above	
"	21/11/16		Embarked in S.S. TEGANTIC 38 officers 890 o.r.	

Army Form C. 21

WAR DIARY
INTELLIGENCE SUMMARY
(Erase heading not required.)

2/14 LOND. R.

Place	Date	Hour	Summary of Events and Information	Remarks and references to Appendices
At sea	29/11/16		At sea	
SALONIKA	10.58 29/11/16		Disembarked at SALONIKA 38 officers 879 other ranks	
			Rifle Guards (Attached)	
			LT COL R.J.L. OGILBY Commanding	
			2/14th Bn. London Regt.	
			MAJOR H.S. CARTWRIGHT. LIEUT. J.S. MONRO. 2nd LT S.E. JONES.	
			" A. BLAIKIE. " L.C.B. BOWKER. " R.D. BAIN.	
			CAPT. R. WHYTE (Adjutant) " D. BLACKWELL. " C.L. WATSON.	
			" D.D. DUNCAN. " T.D.G. MACLAGAN. " W.H. MAIR.	
			" H. BUCHANAN. " R.M. ROBERTSON. " A.S. GINGER.	
			" W. ATTIE LIN. 2nd LT. S.A. PATERSON. LIEUT. P.M. CLEPHANE (Quartermaster)	
			" H. HUNTER. " R.C. HONE.	
			" W.B. LIEBERT. " C.F. BURN.	
			" B. JOBLING. " E. McLEOD.	
			3/4th Bn. Cameron Highlanders (Attached)	
			2nd LT. C.G. MITCHELL 2nd LT. D.H. GOSSIP	
			" W.J. BROWNE. " A. MACDOUGALL.	
			" R.M. CAMERON. " J. TOCHER.	
			" W.J. BETHUNE. " D.W.B. LOW.	
			" G. STILL.	
			4th Res. Bn. Gordon Highlanders (Attached)	
			2nd LT. A. CUTHBERT.	
			" P. GEDDES.	
			" G.A. BUYERS.	
			R.A.M.C.(T) Attached	
			CAPT. I.D. STUBBS.	
			In camp at SALONIKA	
	30/11/16			

www.ingramcontent.com/pod-product-compliance
Lightning Source LLC
Chambersburg PA
CBHW081430160426
43193CB00013B/2243